The Death of the
SAVIOUR

The Death of the
SAVIOUR
Studies in John's Gospel

Richard D. Phillips

THE BANNER OF TRUTH TRUST

THE BANNER OF TRUTH TRUST

3 Murrayfield Road, Edinburgh EH12 6EL, UK
P.O. Box 621, Carlisle, PA 17013, USA

*

© Richard D. Phillips 2012

*

ISBN: 978 1 84871 158 7

*

Typeset in 11/15 Adobe Caslon Pro at
The Banner of Truth Trust, Edinburgh

Printed in the USA by
Versa Press, Inc.,
East Peoria, IL

To
Lydia Margaret Phillips
with all my heart
and
to Him who loves us
and freed us from our sins by His blood
(*Rev.* 1:5)

CONTENTS

PREFACE

What wondrous love is this that caused the Lord of bliss
To bear the dreadful curse for my soul, for my soul?

American folk hymn

THERE can never be enough praise offered, meditation given, or awe experienced about the death of God's Son for our sins. For at the heart of the Christian faith is the simple truth, yet wondrous mystery, that Christ died for us. Realizing this truth changes everything about our lives, which we then offer in willing response to Jesus' sacrifice for us. 'He died for me, so I will live for him', is an aphorism to which the entire Christian faith and experience can be attached. To stand humbly beneath the cross is to be lifted up in adoration over God's love. To live in the shadow of the cross is to walk in the light of Christ's grace and power for salvation. The death of the Saviour is, according to no less an authority than the Apostle Paul, the gospel truth 'of first importance' apart from which we have 'believed in vain' (*1 Cor.* 15:2-3), but through which our faith receives 'the power of God and the wisdom of God' for salvation (*1 Cor.* 1:24).

As a Christian of strongly Reformed convictions, I wish to be known not so much for my doctrines as for a passionate absorption with and in Jesus Christ. Here was the distinction that made

THE DEATH OF THE SAVIOUR

Reformed spiritual giants like John Calvin and the Puritans so mighty in the Lord: not their doctrine alone but their linking of doctrine with doxology. It says much that Calvin's personal motto was not, 'My mind I give to doctrinal study'—though Calvin certainly did that!—but 'My heart I offer to you, O Lord, promptly and sincerely.' The Reformed faith we need to recover today is just that—one composed of doctrinally strong convictions, the aim of which is knowing, communing with, and glorifying our Saviour Jesus Christ.

It is to this end that I offer these studies from John's Gospel on the death of Jesus Christ. Here we discover crystalline doctrine—compressed, clear, and bright—through which we gaze upon the heart of our Lord with wonder and feel the warmth of his grace in our soul. In these biblical texts we may feed from the most sublime of all events ever to transpire in our world: the death of the divine Son whom the Father had sent to save his people. May God bless these brief studies to magnify Christ's saving achievement in our minds, and inspire us to a more fervent adoration of Christ from our hearts.

These studies began life as sermons preached to the congregation of Second Presbyterian Church, Greenville, South Carolina—dear saints to whom I have the enormous privilege of expounding God's Word on a weekly basis. I thank all the beloved members of this church for their prayers and for the support that enables me to devote so much time to study and writing. I especially appreciate my colleagues in ministry, Robert Spears, Gabriel Fluhrer, and Seth Starkey, together with Mr Mel Duncan, apart from whom this labour of love would be too heavy a burden to bear. Even closer to my heart is my thanks to God for my loving wife, Sharon, a true companion, helper, and friend, and for our five children. This volume is dedicated to our youngest child, Lydia Margaret, with fervent prayers that she, like John Calvin, would offer her heart to Jesus, promptly and sincerely. May he who died but lives forever be glorified through God's Word.

RICHARD D. PHILLIPS
Greenville, South Carolina
September 2011

1

KING OF THE JEWS
John 19:13-22

Pilate also wrote an inscription and put it on the cross. It read,
'Jesus of Nazareth, the King of the Jews.' Many of the Jews read
this inscription, for the place where Jesus was crucified was near
the city, and it was written in Aramaic, in Latin, and in Greek (*John*
19:19-20).

J OHN's account of Jesus' arrest and trials differs in many respects
from that of the other Gospels. John seems to see no need to
repeat details recorded elsewhere, omitting such incidents as Si-
mon of Cyrene's help in carrying Jesus' cross (*Matt.* 27:32), Jesus'
warning to the weeping women (*Luke* 23:27-31), the Jews' mocking
of Jesus (*Mark* 15:29-32), the darkness that fell on the land (*Mark*
15:33), Jesus' prayer for his enemies (*Luke* 23:34), the crucified thief's
request for salvation (*Luke* 23:39-43), Jesus' cry of desolation (*Mark*
15:34), the tearing of the curtain in the temple (*Mark* 15:38), and the
centurion's confession of faith (*Mark* 15:39). In the place of these
John adds some remarkable details, including the Jews' objection
to Pilate's inscription (*John* 19:19-22), Jesus' citations from Psalms
22 and 69 (*John* 19:24, 28-29), Jesus committing his mother into
John's hands (*John* 19:25-27), his cry of triumph before death (*John*
19:30), the failure of the soldiers to break his legs (*John* 19:31-33),
and the piercing of Jesus' side with a spear (*John* 19:34). Not only
did John want his eye-witness details to be recorded, but he inserts
them to emphasize his theme of divine sovereignty in the death of
God's Son and Christ's willingness to sacrifice for our sins.

1

THE DEATH OF THE SAVIOUR

The King Renounced

God's sovereignty and Christ's willing submission were the key features of Jesus' trial before Pontius Pilate. The Roman trial has fulfilled God's ancient prophecies (especially those of Isaiah 53) and displayed Jesus' meekness in suffering. It is impossible to obscure, however, the role of Pontius Pilate's corruption of Roman justice and the malice of the Jewish leaders towards their promised Messiah. Pilate had done everything he could, short of courageously performing his duty, to have Jesus released. The Jews, however, were adamant in demanding Jesus' crucifixion and when they threatened to accuse Pilate before Caesar, the governor gave in. He thus concluded the trial in dramatic fashion: 'he brought Jesus out and sat down on the judgment seat at a place called The Stone Pavement, and in Aramaic *Gabbatha*. Now it was the day of Preparation of the Passover. It was about the sixth hour. He said to the Jews, "Behold your King!"' (*John* 19:13-14).

John's citation regarding both the day and the hour has led to disputes among scholars. John places this event on 'the day of the Preparation of the Passover' (*John* 19:14). Some scholars have thought this to designate the day on which the Jews prepared for the Passover, which would have been a Thursday.[1] This view is attractive because, if true, then Jesus, the Lamb of God, was crucified at the very time when the Passover lambs were slaughtered in Jerusalem. There are two problems with this, however. The first is that the other Gospels specify that the Last Supper was the Passover meal (see *Luke* 22:7-8), which was held on the Thursday night, so that Jesus was crucified on the Friday following. Additionally, the word for 'preparation' means the day when preparations were performed in advance of the Sabbath day of rest (see *John* 19:31), which likewise places Jesus' crucifixion on a Friday.[2]

[1] This view is developed in James Montgomery Boice, *The Gospel of John*, 5 vols. (Grand Rapids: Baker, 1999), 5:490-92.
[2] D. A. Carson, *The Gospel of John* (Grand Rapids: Eerdmans, 1991), pp. 603-4.

Even more discussion has resulted from John's statement that Jesus' trial concluded 'about the sixth hour' (*John* 19:14). The problem here is that Mark specifies that 'it was the third hour' when Jesus was crucified. The numerous attempts to reconcile this difference, including the idea that John used a Roman system of time in contrast to Mark's use of Hebrew time, are neither successful nor necessary. We remember that people in those days did not wear watches and did not keep track of minutes and seconds, but gave only approximations. Moreover, in Bible times the day was broken up into four three-hour segments starting at dawn and concluding at sundown. When Mark says that Jesus was crucified in the 'third hour', this probably means some time during the three-hour period begun at the third hour after dawn. John approximates the same time period by saying that Jesus' trial concluded sometime before 'the sixth hour'. John's clarification helps us to see that Mark was referring more generally to late morning instead of specifying 9 a.m. as the time of Jesus' crucifixion. Since we know that darkness covered the land from noon until 3 p.m. (see *Mark* 15:33), this suggests that Jesus was scourged, led with his cross to Golgotha, and nailed to the cross some time in the late morning. Instead of hanging on the cross for three hours before noon (as a reading of Mark alone might suggest), Jesus would have been on the cross a relatively short time before the noon-time darkness began the three-hour torment of his spirit under the wrath of God.

While John notes the time when the trial concluded, he is more concerned with the dialogue between Pilate and the Jews. Having yielded to the crowd's wishes, Pilate brought Jesus to his seat of judgment, which was placed at an elevated area of specially paved stones. Normally, the judge would sit on the throne with the accused before him. But John uses a word that could be translated to say that Pilate sat Jesus on the throne before the people (*John*

19:13). Whether he did this or not, Pilate displayed Jesus, saying, 'Behold your king!' (*John* 19:14).

The irony in John's account is palpable. Just as the faithless high priest Caiaphas unknowingly spoke words in confirmation of Jesus being the atoning sacrifice for the nation—'It is better for you that one man should die for the people' (*John* 11:50)—so also the representative of worldly imperial rule acclaimed the bruised and bloodied Jesus as king. God thus hailed his Son as the Saviour-King through the very lips of those who conspired unjustly to crucify him.

If Pilate's presentation of Jesus was ironic, the cry of the assembled Jews plumbed new depths of tragedy. 'They cried out, "Away with him, away with him, crucify him!"' If this were not madness enough, Pilate made one last appeal: 'Shall I crucify your King?' To this, the chief priests answered, 'We have no king but Caesar' (*John* 19:15). So intent were these false and self-serving shepherds on having a Messiah of their own making and a righteousness for their own boasting that they rejected the Saviour-King whom God had sent. In despising Jesus, they renounced their sacred covenant with God, repudiating the principle at the heart of Israel's life from the beginning, namely, that God is himself King over his people. In God's place they pledged allegiance to a vile Gentile ruler. George Beasley-Murray comments that this renunciation of Jesus 'is nothing less than the abandonment of the messianic hope of Israel... their repudiation of the promise of the kingdom of God, with which the gift of the Messiah is inseparably bound in Jewish faith'.

The Jews show that in rejecting Jesus one cannot avoid losing his or her soul. In earthly terms, those who hear but refuse to receive Jesus' gospel, like these Jewish leaders who refused to humble themselves as sinners before God's throne of mercy, consign themselves to a life of increasing darkness. It may be the darkness of a Christless morality, a lifestyle of proud and graceless rebellion to God's gospel rule. Or, more frequently, it may be the darkness of an increasing descent into immoral wretchedness. In the case of the Jews, their rejection of Jesus led to the pride and folly that ultimately ended in Jerusalem's destruction at the pitiless hands of the Roman master they had called upon to rid them of Jesus.

Even worse are the *eternal* implications of renouncing the crucified Jesus as Saviour and King. The Jews likely thought they were making a meaningless gesture by acclaiming their loyalty to Caesar, whom they actually despised. Yet their words were recorded in heaven. Paul would later explain that 'being ignorant of the righteousness of God, and seeking to establish their own, they did not submit to God's righteousness' (*Rom.* 10:3). As a result, God's ancient people, to whom the Lord had held out his arms for salvation through all the rolling centuries, put themselves in the position formerly occupied by the hated Gentiles: 'strangers to the covenants of promise, having no hope and without God in the world' (*Eph.* 2:12).

How unreasonable was the Jews' rejection of Jesus, when their own Scriptures so plainly pointed forward to him! Yet it is equally unreasonable for people to refuse Jesus today, and with equally tragic results. How many people, thoughtlessly blaspheming the name of God's Son or flippantly casting aside the gospel offer of salvation, likewise consign their immortal souls to a just and eternal punishment? God has presented his crucified Son yet his grace is contemptuously rejected. As the writer of Hebrews warned, 'how shall we escape if we neglect such a great salvation?' (*Heb.* 2:3).

The King Crucified

John's account of what happened next is as brief and direct as the event is epochal: 'So [Pilate] delivered him over to them to be crucified' (*John* 19:16). With this statement, John introduces the most important event in human history. Mark Johnson writes:

> It is for this moment that the whole of the Bible has been preparing us. From the time of the Fall, throughout the whole Old Testament revelation, God was leading his people towards that day when he would send a Saviour and through him bring about salvation for all time. Similarly, from the moment of the conception of Jesus in the womb of the virgin Mary, right through to the climax of his ministry in Jerusalem, the Gospels have been preparing us for this—his death, and everything that it would achieve.[3]

In approaching Jesus' crucifixion, we should observe that John gives little attention to the grisly details of the physical suffering experienced. This contrasts with popular treatments of Christ's death, which often seek to stir up the emotions with lurid details of what Jesus suffered. Neither John nor any of the other Gospels follow this approach. Admittedly, however, when the apostles mentioned the crucifixion, their original audiences understood a good deal of what this involved, many of them having witnessed such dreadful spectacles. This warrants us surveying the likely sequence of events in Jesus' crucifixion.

John writes that Pilate delivered Jesus 'over to them', meaning that he consented to the people's wish. A squad of Roman soldiers would then have seized Jesus, and it is likely that he now received the *verberatio*, the savage scourging with the Roman whip that rent his flesh almost to the point of death. John continues: 'they took Jesus, and he went out, bearing his own cross, to the place called the place of a skull, which in Aramaic is called Golgotha. There they crucified him, and with him two others, one on either side, and Jesus between them' (*John* 19:16-18).

A crucifixion was terrible to behold. William Barclay states that 'the Romans themselves regarded it with a shudder of horror. Cicero declared that it was "the most cruel and horrifying death".

[3] Mark Johnson, *Let's Study John* (Edinburgh: Banner of Truth, 2003), p. 246.

Tacitus said that it was a "despicable death".[4] For this reason, no Roman citizen could be crucified for any crime, this form of execution being typically reserved for slaves and rebels. Death by crucifixion it seems was invented by the Persians, imported to the Mediterranean by the Carthaginians, and perfected by the Romans. Its basic feature was to combine shame with physical anguish, as the sufferer hung in the air slowly and tortuously to die.

The scourging that preceded the crucifixion was so brutal that many victims did not survive it. It is apparently because of the loss of blood that Jesus suffered through the violence of his beating, as recorded in the other Gospels, that he collapsed under the weight of his cross. John, keen to emphasize Jesus' self-mastery, points out that Jesus began by 'bearing his own cross' (*John* 19:17). After his fairly long ordeal in traversing the so-called *Via Dolorosa* (the 'Way of Sorrows'), Jesus arrived at the place of crucifixion outside the city walls. Typically, the prisoner carried only his cross-beam, the vertical beam having been set in place in advance. John identifies the place of execution as 'the place of a skull, which in Aramaic is called Golgotha'. The Latin for 'place of the skull' is Calvary. We do not know what accounts for this name, and though many have assumed that Jesus was crucified on a skull-shaped hill, neither Scripture nor early church tradition validates this notion.

Once at Golgotha, Jesus' hands or wrists were nailed to the cross-beam, and when he was lifted up his feet were nailed to the vertical post of the cross. Crucifixion victims often died of asphixiation or slowly expired by exposure and the loss of blood. The pressure of the body's weight on the nailed feet resulting from the victim's attempt to fills his lungs with breath must have been excruciating.

Even this brief description shows that Jesus suffered unspeakable agony in dying for our sins. Yet his shocking physical suffering paled

[4] William Barclay, *The Gospel of John*, 2 vols. (Philadelphia, PA: Westminster, 1975), 2:291.

in comparison to the outpouring of God's wrath upon Jesus' soul. It was Jesus' spiritual horror that prompted his cry of desolation, summing up the anguish of his spiritual alienation from the Father: 'My God, my God, why have you forsaken me?' (*Matt.* 27:46).

The details that John chose to highlight are undoubtedly significant to his message. First, Jesus was taken outside the city to die, just as the Israelites had for centuries cast away the remains of the sin-offerings outside the walls. This was especially the case for the sin-offering on the annual Day of Atonement. Leviticus 16:27 specifies that these carcasses be disposed outside the camp, which anticipated the fulfilment of this ordinance in the crucifixion of Jesus Christ outside the city.

The writer of Hebrews would later exhort Christ's followers to 'go to him outside the camp and bear the reproach he endured' (*Heb.* 13:13), which meant departing from the external rituals of Judaism in order to receive the benefits of Christ's spiritual sacrifice. So it has been since the earliest days of our faith. History records the words of England's Archbishop Laud, the champion of lofty rituals and religious show, when he visited Scotland in 1633 and found no great cathedrals or other displays of religious grandeur. Laud scoffed that the poor people had 'no religion at all that I could see—which grieved me much'.⁵ What Laud did not notice was that outside the camp of religious formalism the believing Scots had Christ and his atoning blood by faith alone. Christians continue to go to Christ's cross outside the camp, bearing the world's scorn for Jesus. We do not need staged worship experiences, dancing fountains, or any other item of religious paraphernalia so common today to be saved. Rather, eternal life is received when from the heart we embrace the cross of Christ through simple faith in God's Word.

Second, as Jesus carries the cross, John undoubtedly sees God's

⁵ Cited from F. F. Bruce, *Hebrews* (Grand Rapids, MI: Eerdmans, 1990), p. 379.

covenant curse for our sins resting on Christ's holy shoulders. From the time of the early church, Christians have drawn a link between Jesus carrying his cross and Abraham's son, Isaac, carrying the wood on his back for the sacrifice that was to be offered on Mount Moriah. In that great story found in Genesis 22, Isaac asked his father the question that in many ways summed up the longing of the entire Old Testament: 'Behold, the fire and the wood, but where is the lamb for a burnt offering?' Abraham answered the question with a faith that looked to the future: 'God will provide for himself the lamb for a burnt offering, my son' (*Gen.* 22:7-8). When father and son arrived atop Mount Moriah, Abraham laid his son upon the altar in obedience to God's command. However, as Abraham prepared to plunge the knife into his son, an angel intervened to stop him. And there stuck in a nearby thicket was a ram—a sacrifice instead of Isaac, a substitute provided by God (*Gen.* 22:12-13). Now, in a far more glorious way, Jesus takes not only Isaac's place but the place of every believing sinner whose guilt required nothing less than death upon the altar of God's holy justice. On the cross 'the Lamb of God takes away the sin of the world' (*John* 1:29). God provides the sacrifice to free us from our sins.

Third, not only was Jesus led outside the city walls carrying his cross, but once at the place of execution he was crucified between two others. John writes: 'There they crucified him, and with him two others, one on either side, and Jesus between them' (*John* 19:18). The other Gospels inform us that these men were condemned as thieves, or perhaps more accurately as insurrectionists (possibly associates of Barabbas). John's point in drawing our attention to these criminals is to point out the fulfilment of Isaiah 53:12: 'he poured out his soul to death and was numbered with the transgressors'. The Romans were probably meaning to shame Jesus further by placing the Jewish King between two others who were dying for the crimes of which Jesus had been accused but acquitted.

Without doubt John wants us to see the glorious significance of Christ's atoning death. All through his ministry Jesus had been scoffed at for associating with sinners, yet he replied, 'I came not to call the righteous, but sinners' (*Mark* 2:17). It was only appropriate, therefore, for Jesus to be crucified between guilty wrongdoers. Leon Morris writes:

> For the writers of the Gospels this was not an insult but the expression of an important truth. Jesus came to save sinners. He died to save them, and the fact that on the cross he hung between people who were obviously grievous sinners graphically illustrated that truth. His death was a death on behalf of sinners, and his position when he died brought that out for those who had eyes to see.[6]

The King Acclaimed

John's account of the crucifixion emphasizes God's sovereignty and Jesus' mastery in submitting himself to death. So far, however, everything seems to have gone against Jesus. But John adds a detail that reminds us of God's control over every detail in this event and reveals Jesus' glory shining through his cross. We see this in the placard inscribed by Pontius Pilate, which acclaimed Jesus' kingship even in the agony of his crucifixion. John recounts: 'Pilate also wrote an inscription and put it on the cross. It read "Jesus of Nazareth, the King of the Jews"' (*John* 19:19).

Never wanting to miss the deterrent effect of a crucifixion, the Roman practice was to write out the criminal's offence on a tablet, called a *titlos,* that would be paraded in front of the victim as he carried his cross to the place of execution. So it was that Pilate, having personally examined the accused, Jesus of Nazareth, directed that he be identified as the King of the Jews. In this action, we may be sure that the hand of God was ruling so that the honour

[6] Leon Morris, *Reflections on the Gospel of John* (Peabody, MA: Hendrickson, 1986), p. 658.

of his Son would be made plainly known. Beasley-Murray writes, 'Pilate, the judge and representative of the dominion that ruled the world, hereby declares that Jesus on his cross is King of his people.'[7] A king conquers, provides, rules, and makes peace. Christ our King conquered our enemy the devil, provided forgiveness for our sins, rules in our hearts, and makes peace between sinners and God. All of these kingly deeds Jesus achieved by dying on the cross for us, so it is proper for him to have been hailed as king there.

Recent scholarship has indicated that the *titlos* was normally carried to the place of execution but not affixed to the cross. Thus it was by God's special arrangement that the placard accusing Jesus of his kingship was placed above him as he suffered, so that passers-by would learn the reason for his death. John writes, 'Many of the Jews read this inscription, for the place where Jesus was crucified was near the city, and it was written in Aramaic, in Latin, and in Greek' (*John* 19:20). Hebrew was the language of God's revelation,[8] Latin was the language of power, and Greek was the language of wisdom. Matthew Henry comments: 'In each of these languages Christ is proclaimed King, in whom are hid all the treasures of revelation, wisdom, and power.'[9]

A week earlier, Jesus had exclaimed, 'The hour has come for the Son of Man to be glorified... And I, when I am lifted up from the earth, will draw all people to myself' (*John* 12:23; 12:32). Now, just as he had said, Israel's king and the world's Saviour was lifted up along the highway of Jerusalem and hailed before the eyes of all. By noting the three languages in which Jesus' kingship was declared, a detail which John alone notes, the apostle is stating that 'Jesus is a King for everyone. He is not

---

[7] Beasley-Murray, *John*, p. 346.

[8] While many scholars believe John 19:20 refers to Aramaic, the Greek text states that the sign was written in Hebrew, as well as Latin and Greek.

[9] Matthew Henry, *Commentary on the Whole Bible*, 6 vols. (Peabody, MA: Hendrickson, n.d.), 5:967.

merely a Jewish Saviour, though he is that. He is the Saviour of the Greeks and of the Romans as well. He is the Saviour of the world.'[10]

Predictably, the Jewish leaders were incensed by Pilate's inscription as it was paraded before the cross and then affixed above the suffering body of Jesus. Their anger is easily understood, since the sign declared both the innocence of the man they had cruelly betrayed and their treason against God. Never lacking for cunning, they suggested only a small addition, 'Do not write, "The King of the Jews", but rather, "This man said, I am King of the Jews"' (*John* 19:21). For once, however, Pilate was obstinate: 'What I have written I have written', he answered (*John* 19:22). It was God's will that truly would not be altered, and God's declaration of the righteousness, glory, and dominion of his Son can never be annulled by the indignant unbelief of rebellious mankind. Thus was established the true cause of Jesus' death: he died because he was King of God's covenant nation and because only through his death could his beloved but sinful people be forgiven and enter eternal life. As John stated in the first verse of his account of Jesus' passion, 'having loved his own who were in the world, he loved them to the end' (*John* 13:1).

Hailing the King

As we reflect on the religious leaders' reaction to the sign identifying Jesus as King of the Jews, we see that the cross not only declares God's saving grace to the world but also reveals the state of human hearts. The chief priests' objection to Pilate's sign shows how hardened and dark their hearts had become since they would not humble themselves as sinners before God. As Paul later explained, to such people the cross exudes only the aroma of death. But there are others for whom the cross spreads 'a fragrance from

[10] Boice, *John*, 5:1502.

life to life' (*2 Cor.* 2:16). One such person was one of the men crucified with Jesus, whose salvation John probably intends for us to recall from the other Gospels. At first, both thieves reviled Jesus along with the bystanders. But one of them, reflecting on his approaching death and perceiving Jesus' majesty as the King of the Jews, called out to Jesus for salvation. 'Jesus', he pleaded, 'remember me when you come into your kingdom.' Jesus answered with a royal decree of grace from the cross, 'Truly, I say to you, today you will be with me in Paradise' (*Luke* 23:42-43).

Can you give any justifiable reason why you should not do the same? Why should you not hail Jesus as the true King of glory, the sinless Saviour who died out of love for you, gaining your forgiveness by bearing the curse of your sins on the cross? Should you refuse to call on Jesus for salvation, you will be joining the Jewish leaders in preferring to be damned forever rather than humble yourself in submission to Jesus and his cross. C. H. Spurgeon appeals to us all:

> He claims to be King, so stand at the foot of the cross, I pray you, and admit his claim. If you would have Jesus to be your Saviour, you must have him as your King; you must submit to his government, for he claims the right to rule over all who acknowledge him to be Jesus; yea more than that, he claims to rule all mankind, for all power is given unto him in heaven and in earth, and we are bidden to proclaim his kingdom throughout the whole world, and to say to all men, 'Jesus of Nazareth is your King, bow down before him . . . The claims of Christ . . . were published even from the tree on which he died; so do not resist them, but willingly yield yourselves up to Jesus now, and let him be King to you henceforth and for ever.'[11]

[11] C. H. Spurgeon, *Metropolitan Tabernacle Pulpit*, 63 vols. (London: Passmore & Alabaster, 1908), 54:608.

2

BENEATH THE CROSS
John 19:23-27

This was to fulfil the Scripture which says, 'They divided my garments among them, and for my clothing they cast lots' (*John* 19:24).

ONE of the most important principles for interpreting the Bible is to recognize its Christ-centred character. This principle does not mean that every passage in the Bible must be forced to make a direct reference to Jesus, whether one is present or not. It does mean that the message of the Bible as a whole is directed to the person and work of Jesus Christ. Therefore, every passage in the Bible, whatever its content, should be interpreted within the context of the Bible's overall Christ-centred message. This is the interpretive principle taught by Jesus himself. In John 5, Jesus expressed dismay at the Jewish leaders' refusal to believe on him, since they were students of the Scriptures and, Jesus insisted, 'it is they that bear witness about me' (*John* 5:39). In Jesus' famous conversation with the Emmaus Road disciples on the day of the resurrection, Jesus opened the Scriptures and 'beginning with Moses and all the Prophets, he interpreted to them in all the Scriptures the things concerning himself' (*Luke* 24:27).

The recognition of the Bible's central focus on salvation through Jesus Christ was a key principle of the Protestant Reformation. Martin Luther emphasized this point, writing:

He, *He,* Mary's Son, is the one who is able to give eternal life to all who come to Him and believe on Him. Therefore he who would correctly and profitably read Scripture should see to it that he finds Christ in it; then he finds life eternal without fail. On the other hand, if I do not so study and understand Moses and the prophets so as to find that Christ came from Heaven for the sake of my salvation, became man, suffered, died, was buried, rose, and ascended to Heaven so that through Him I enjoy reconciliation with God, forgiveness of all my sins, grace, righteousness, and life eternal, then my reading in Scripture is of no help whatsoever to my salvation.[1]

James Boice comments of this: 'Luther's point is that the Scriptures are, both in their general outline and in specific details, God's Word to us about Jesus. It is undoubtedly this keen spiritual insight that made him the tower of strength and the winsome exegete that he was. Luther believed that the Bible was God's Word and that it was about Jesus. Consequently, whenever he approached the Bible, he knew from the start who was speaking in it and what its theme was.'[2]

Lots for Christ's Clothing

One way in which the Old Testament pointed to Jesus was through the prophecies that were fulfilled at his cross. These prophecies served the dual purpose of proving that Jesus died according to God's foreordained plan and of providing the Bible's interpretation of Jesus' death as an atoning sacrifice for sin. The apostle John was keen to point out the fulfilment of prophecy in Jesus' death, explicitly noting four of them. Working backwards from the last one, John points out that Jesus' side was pierced by

---

[1] Martin Luther, *What Luther Says*, vol. 1, comp. Ewald M. Plass (St. Louis: Concordia, 1959), pp. 69-70.
[2] James Montgomery Boice, *The Gospel of John*, 5 vols. (Grand Rapids: Baker, 1999), 5:1508.

a spear in fulfilment of Zechariah 12:10 (*John* 19:37); Jesus' bones were left unbroken, as was foretold in Psalm 34:20 (*John* 19:36); before dying Jesus gasped, 'I thirst,' fulfilling Psalm 69:21 (*John* 19:28); and after crucifying Jesus the Roman soldiers gambled for his clothes. John writes: 'When the soldiers had crucified Jesus, they took his garments and divided them into four parts, one part for each soldier; also his tunic. But the tunic was seamless, woven in one piece from top to bottom, so they said to one another, "Let us not tear it, but cast lots for it to see whose it shall be." This was to fulfil the Scripture which says, "They divided my garments among them, and for my clothing they cast lots." So the soldiers did these things' (*John* 19:23-24). This dividing of Jesus' clothing and casting of lots for the final piece fulfilled Psalm 22:18, 'they divide my garments among them, and for my clothing they cast lots.'

It was apparently the standard Roman practice for the soldiers who performed an execution to take the victim's clothing. Scholars state that the average Jew of Jesus' time wore five articles of clothing: a loincloth, a tunic, shoes, a turban or scarf, and an outer robe. Since there were four soldiers, this permitted one article for each, with the outer garment left over. Normally, the robe would be torn apart at the seams and the pieces distributed, except that Jesus' robe was 'seamless, woven in one piece from top to bottom'. There was no point tearing it up, so the soldiers decided to cast lots to see who would take the robe. This shows that while the soldiers had no notion of fulfilling ancient prophecy, God was exercising his sovereign control through their otherwise pointless actions. Just as Pontius Pilate had unknowingly published the truth about Jesus when he ordered that his placard declare him the 'King of the Jews', so also the soldiers' thoughtless action pointed out Jesus as the true David of Psalm 22 who suffers humiliation for God's people.

Many Bible interpreters have imagined an allegorical significance to Jesus' seamless robe beyond anything stated by the text. The early church scholar Origen saw in it the wholeness of Christ's teaching, Cyprian saw it depicting the unity of the church, and Cyril saw it representing Christ's virgin birth.[3] Roman Catholic apologists touted Christ's seamless garment as symbolic of the church which should not be divided, accusing Luther and the other Reformers of 'rending the seamless tunic' of Christ.[4] Some Reformed writers have also allegorized Christ's seamless garment, seeing it as a picture of Christ's perfect imputed righteousness. Noting the tendency for gross subjectivism in such allegories, we do better to avoid altogether this kind of interpretation when not specifically warranted by the text.

This does not mean, however, that there is no clear meaning to the dividing of Jesus' garments. This episode dramatized the certainty of Jesus' death once he was crucified, since it is dead men whose clothes were distributed. Moreover, the casting of lots for Jesus' clothing signified his humiliation in death, as Jesus' final possessions were carelessly handled by the men who had put him to death.

Perhaps most significant is the clear implication that Jesus was stripped naked in his crucifixion. Romans stripped their enemies and victims to shame them, and Jesus' nakedness in death was one way in which he offered himself as our substitute. The shame of nakedness is part of the curse for our sin. Adam and Eve in the Garden were naked and without shame because of their original righteousness (*Gen.* 2:25). But after they fell into sin, their nakedness was a source of shame and they sought to cover themselves with fig leaves (*Gen.* 3:7). Therefore, just as Jesus bore the thorns of sin's curse (*Gen.*

---

[3]Leon Morris, *Reflections on the Gospel of John* (Peabody, Mass.: Hendrickson, 1986), p. 664.
[4]Gordon J. Keddie, *A Study Commentary on John*, 2 vols. (Darlington: Evangelical Press, 2001), 2:336.

3:18) in his mocking crown, he also bore the reproach of our nakedness in his death.

Christians should rejoice in this glorious gospel provision, especially those who are tormented in shame for their own sins or for sins that others have committed against them. Jesus in his death bore not only the guilt but also the shame of sin. Isaiah foresaw Jesus dying with our reproach upon him, saying that 'as one from whom men hide their faces he was despised' (*Isa.* 53:3). Therefore none who come to God in Jesus' name need ever be ashamed, since Jesus has borne our shame and removed all disgrace from those he saves.

It is in this way that we rightly relate the imputed righteousness of Christ to this scene at the cross. Jesus bore our sin not only to remove our guilt and shame but also to clothe us with his righteousness. Paul explained, 'For our sake [God] made him to be sin who knew no sin, so that in him we might become the righteousness of God' (*2 Cor.* 5:21). John Calvin explains: 'Christ was stripped of his garments, that he might clothe us with righteousness; his naked body was exposed to the insults of men, that we may appear in glory before the judgment-seat of God.'5 Through faith in Christ our sin is placed onto his cross and our nakedness is clothed in the white robes of his righteousness, that we sinners might stand unashamed before God.

Psalm 22 and the Torment of the Cross

I pointed out that the fulfilment of Psalm 22:18 in the casting of lots for Jesus' clothing identifies him as the true David who suffers for God's people. There is good reason to believe that Psalm 22, which David wrote to lament his own sufferings as God's anointed shepherd, details the anguished experience of Jesus during the three hours that he suffered on the cross.

5John Calvin, *Calvin's Commentaries*, 23 vols. (Grand Rapids: Baker, 1848, reprint 2009), 18:230.

THE DEATH OF THE SAVIOUR

Mark's Gospel tells us that at the sixth hour, noon, a supernatural darkness fell upon the land, obscuring the spiritual torment of Jesus as he bore our sins under God's wrath (*Mark* 15:33). This continued for three hours, until at the ninth hour Jesus surrendered his spirit and died. John's reference to the fulfilment of Psalm 22 identifies Jesus as the one who fulfils the suffering of David's psalm. Moreover, we should note that the first and the last of Jesus' seven sayings on the cross are taken from Psalm 22. Matthew tells us that when the time of darkness had almost expired, Jesus cried out, 'My God, my God, why have you forsaken me?' (*Matt.* 27:46). This cites the opening words of Psalm 22. Then, just before yielding his spirit into the Father's hands, Jesus quoted from the end of Psalm 22. David says, 'They shall come and proclaim his righteousness to a people yet unborn', and then concludes the psalm saying, 'he has done it' (*Psa.* 22:31). This last statement can be translated in the way that Jesus states it in John 19:30, 'It is finished.'

Since Jesus responded to his sufferings on the cross by citing the beginning and the end of Psalm 22, it is likely that the psalm as a whole depicts the flow of Jesus' experience during the crucifixion. We can outline this flow in three points: Jesus was forsaken, Jesus was crushed, and Jesus was executed.

Psalm 22 expresses how Christ was *forsaken* by noting God's refusal to deliver him: 'All who see me mock me; they make mouths at me; they wag their heads; "He trusts in the Lord; let him deliver him, let him rescue him, for he delights in him!"' (*Psa.* 22:7-8). This was precisely the taunt thrown in Jesus' face during his crucifixion. Matthew records: 'So also the chief priests, with the scribes and elders, mocked him, saying, "He saved others,; he cannot save himself... He trusts in God; let God deliver him now, if he desires him. For he said, "I am the Son of God"' (*Matt.* 27:41-43). That God did not deliver Jesus from the cross, but abandoned his Son to suffer all the torment of his wrath on our sins, shows how Jesus suffered as one truly abandoned by God in his death.

Second, Psalm 22 speaks of Jesus being *crushed* on the cross: 'I am a worm and not a man, scorned by mankind and despised by the people' (*Psa.* 22:6). It may seem bizarre to us for Jesus to compare himself to a worm. But this expression in Jesus' time had come to refer to a certain kind of worm, the *tola*, from whose blood a valuable crimson dye was made. To release the dye, the animal was crushed, so that its blood would flow out. James Boice comments: 'This image throws light upon Christ's thoughts, for when Jesus thought of himself as the *tola*, he thought of himself as the worm who is *crushed* for God's people. His blood was shed for us that we might be clothed in bright raiment.'[6] This perfectly accords with the prophecy of Isaiah 53:10: 'it was the will of the LORD to crush him; he has put him to grief.' In shedding his blood, therefore, Jesus submitted his soul to be crushed as he suffered under God's wrath on the cross for us.

Third, the bulk of Psalm 22 is devoted to David's grief over those who were determined to see him dead. Likewise, Jesus knew himself as one who was *executed* on the cross. 'Many bulls encompass me; strong bulls of Bashan surround me' the psalm laments; 'they open wide their mouths at me, like a ravening and roaring lion' (*Psa.* 22:12-13). Further threats include the sword, the mouth of the lion, and the horns of the wild oxen (*Psa.* 22:20-21). The wild oxen is especially significant as an animal on which victims were sometimes bound for execution. Jesus, following the pathos of this psalm, suffered by reflecting on the judicial aspect of his execution, knowing full well that he was judicially executed as he bore the sins we have committed.

Jesus' Family Matters

John does not dwell on Jesus' sufferings beyond referring us to Psalm 22, instead placing his focus beneath the cross. First, he

---

[6] Boice, *John*, 5:1511.

told us of the soldiers who cast lots for his robe. In John 19:25-27 he then identifies four women who were present out of love for Jesus: 'standing by the cross of Jesus were his mother and his mother's sister, Mary the wife of Clopas, and Mary Magdalene' (*John* 19:25).

It is not entirely clear how to understand this list of women. As some see it, John names two women only, first specifying them as Jesus' mother and her sister, and then giving their names as 'Mary the wife of Clopas and Mary Magdalene.' There is no indication elsewhere, however, that Jesus' mother had remarried after the death of Joseph or that Mary Magdalene was her sister. Others see three women identified, with John saying that Mary's sister was 'Mary the wife of Clopas.' It is difficult to imagine two sisters with the same name, however, so it is probably best to take John as identifying four women. The first two are identified as Jesus' mother Mary and her sister, accompanied by Mary the wife of Clopas and Mary Magdalene. When we compare this list with that of Mark's Gospel, this indicates that Mary the wife of Clopas was the mother of Jesus' disciples 'James the younger and of Joses.' More interesting still is that Mark names the fourth woman as Salome and Matthew notes that she was 'the mother of the sons of Zebedee' (*Matt.* 27:56), that is, the mother of the apostle John and his brother James. Since Mark specifies that there were other unnamed women in the vicinity of the cross, this identification of the fourth woman is far from certain. If this interpretation is correct, however, it makes the apostle John the cousin of Jesus Christ according to the flesh. This might account in part for the close bond between them and also for Jesus' decision to commit his mother's care to John.

Among these four women, it was Jesus' mother who drew his attention and should draw ours as well. Thirty years earlier, when she and her husband Joseph had presented Jesus at the temple aged twelve, Simeon had blessed the child but then spoke words of warning to the young mother, saying that 'a sword will pierce through your own soul' (*Luke* 2:35). Did Mary think of those words as their reality struck with the force that only a mother watching her son die can know? Standing steadfast by Jesus, Mary continues the example of virtue for which her memory should be prized by all her brothers and sisters in Christ.

If Mary was faithful to her son to the end, Jesus in response acted out of concern for her even in such an hour of darkness for himself. John records that there was a fifth friend of Jesus present beneath the cross, namely, himself. To John, Jesus committed the care of his earthly mother: 'When Jesus saw his mother and the disciple whom he loved standing nearby, he said to his mother, "Woman, behold, your son!" Then he said to the disciple, "Behold, your mother!" And from that hour the disciple took her to his own home' (*John* 19:26-27).

Jesus' concern for Mary's welfare is one more instance of his compassion and concern for all in need, even amidst such physical and spiritual agony. Jesus had made provision for his murderers, praying for the Father to forgive them (*Luke* 23:34). Jesus had provided for the penitent thief who asked to be remembered in Jesus' kingdom, promising him to be in paradise that very day (*Luke* 23:43). Now Jesus attended to the needs of his mother.

Jesus ministered to Mary in two important ways. First, he addressed her not as 'Mother' but as 'Woman'. Some commentators have speculated that Jesus was seeking to spare Mary the grief of hearing her son calling upon her as his mother. But the clear and important significance of this way of speaking is that Jesus was alerting Mary to her need to relate to him not as a mother but as a member of that fallen race of Adam and Eve. The greatest mistake for even a spiritually-minded person like Jesus' mother Mary is to seek a claim on Jesus through the merits of the flesh. J. C. Ryle comments:

> Henceforth she must daily remember, that her first aim must be to live the life of faith as a believing woman, like all other Christian women. Her blessedness did not consist in being related to Christ according to the flesh, but in believing and keeping Christ's Word.[7]

Having called his mother to faith in him as Lord and Saviour, Jesus then made provision for her temporal care after his departure. 'Woman, behold, your son!' Jesus said, directing Mary to the care of the disciple John. 'Behold, your mother!' he told John (*John* 19:26-27). The apostle concludes, 'And from that hour the disciple took her to his own home' (*John* 19:27). Scripture does not record Mary's future life, but tradition states that Mary lived with John in Jerusalem for eleven more years until she died or, in an alternative version, that she travelled with John to Ephesus in later years and died there.[8]

Roman Catholic theologians have made this passage a centrepiece of their teaching of Mary as co-redemptrix along with her son, Jesus. Such a doctrine can only be gleaned from this text by turning Jesus' words on their head. Whereas Jesus plainly commits his mother to the care of his beloved disciple, Roman Catholics insist that Jesus was committing the apostles and the church into the care of his mother. Some go so far as to say that Jesus sees this installment of Mary over the church as his ultimate achievement on the cross. It is true that Jesus entrusted his church into the care of another, but his farewell discourse of the previous night made clear that this other was the Holy Spirit. 'I will ask the Father, and he will give you another Helper', Jesus said, referring not to his earthly

---

[7] Ryle, *John*, 3:51-2.
[8] Frederick Louis Godet, *Commentary on the Gospel of John* (Grand Rapids: Zondervan, 1893), 3:387.

mother but to 'the Spirit of truth', who 'will be with you forever' (*John* 14:16,17).

Jesus' care for his mother does set an important example for us in our attentiveness to the needs of our parents in their elderly years. Jesus was faithful to fulfil the fifth commandment, which commands us to honour our father and mother (*Exod.* 20:12). But even as Jesus fulfils this commandment, he shows us that the spiritual family of believers is more significant than the blood relations of our earthly families. Mary had other sons, we know, but they had not yet believed on Jesus, so our Lord commits his mother not into their care but into the care of one who will have a spiritual, as well as material, interest in Mary's care. On the cross, Jesus was bringing together a new family by means of his atoning blood, and this spiritual family of God's born-again children is more important to Jesus than other earthly ties (see also *Luke* 8:21; 14:26). Jesus' concern for his mother did not deter him from fulfilling the redeeming work God gave him to do, and while children are urged by his example to attend to the needs of their parents, we should not be deterred from serving the Lord solely because of family considerations.

The Faithful Saviour

In recounting the crucifixion, John labours to highlight Jesus' faithfulness. Jesus was faithful to God in fulfilling the prophecies of Scripture to the letter, voluntarily undergoing abandonment, crushing violence, and a shameful execution so that God's saving plan might be fulfilled. Jesus was faithful to his mother, providing for her needs even while he suffered on the cross. Finally, Jesus was faithful to us as he bore our nakedness in sin, shed his crimson blood to cleanse us of our guilt, and provided the righteousness we need to stand in favour before God. The cross brings the message of the whole Bible into focus, showing that God has fulfilled his promised offer of salvation through the gift of his crucified Son to die, who would rise from the dead in everlasting resurrection power. God the Father and God the Son have been faithful to their saving promises: will you have faith in them, thereby entering God's family through the gift of Christ's sin-atoning sacrifice?

The only conceivable reasons to refuse Jesus are those of the Jewish leaders and the Roman soldiers. The Jews wanted to be justified by their own righteousness, despite their obvious sins, so they reviled Jesus on the cross. The Romans were more interested in worldly riches, even the poor articles of Jesus' clothing, which they happily gathered while neglecting the righteousness he gives to those who believe. To the self-righteous, the Bible says, 'God opposes the proud, but gives grace to the humble' (*James* 4:6). To the worldly and greedy, Jesus warns against the folly of seeking after riches but neglecting the higher matter of salvation. Jesus' cross declares that the great need of everyone living on earth—from a supposed saint like Mary to the calloused Roman soldiers who crucified Jesus—is salvation from the sins that otherwise condemn us before God, a salvation available to all through faith in Christ.

We have seen that Psalm 22 seemed to chronicle Jesus' experience during his torment on the cross. If that is true, then the conclusion to the psalm tells us that the salvation of sinners was the main thought in Jesus' mind as he looked on all those gathered beneath his cross. The psalm's final verse says: 'They shall come and proclaim his righteousness to a people yet unborn, that he has done it' (*Psa.* 22:30-31). This righteousness of Christ that we proclaim today can be yours if you will stand beneath his cross, look to Jesus in faith, and yield to him the fidelity of your heart. Then the psalm of Jesus' cross will have been fulfilled in you when it says that 'those who seek him shall praise the LORD!' (*Psa.* 22:26).

3

THE DEATH OF THE SAVIOUR
John 19:28-30

After this, Jesus, knowing that all was now finished, said (to fulfil the Scripture), 'I thirst' (*John* 19:28).

C HRISTIANITY is different from every other religion in its utter dependence on its founder. Jesus is uniquely linked to Christianity in the sense that there is no Christianity at all without him. This situation does not exist in any other religion. Buddhism and Confucianism rely on teachings that are ascribed to their founders but could have come from any other source. The men themselves are not necessary, but only their ideas. The same is true even of Islam in its relationship to Muhammad. While Muslims point to Muhammad as the recipient of the supposed revelation that came from the Archangel Gabriel, the person and life of Muhammad himself are not necessary to the beliefs taught in the Qur'an.

In contrast, Christianity is a set of beliefs about Jesus himself. John Stott explained: 'The person and work of Christ are the rock upon which the Christian religion is built. If he is not who he said he was, and if he did not do what he said he had come to do, the foundation is undermined and the whole superstructure will collapse. Take Christ from Christianity, and you disembowel it; there is practically nothing left. Christ is the center of Christianity; all else is circumference.'[1]

Not only does Christianity require belief in the person and work of Christ, but our faith involves a personal relationship with Jesus

[1]John R. W. Stott, *Basic Christianity* (Downers Grove, IL: InterVarsity Press, 1971), p. 21.

as he continues to live and reign today. Jesus Christ is himself the substance of Christian faith and life.

When it comes to Jesus' saving work, the Christian faith centers on his sin-atoning death, to which we now come in John's Gospel. I intend to consider the death of Jesus in three studies, in which we will examine the *fact* of Jesus' death as a substitute for sinners, the *results* of Jesus' death in atoning for our sin, and then the *finality* of Jesus' death, as seen in his triumphant cry, 'It is finished' (*John* 19:30).

Jesus' Cry of Thirst

When Christians believe in Jesus, we confess that he is both truly God and truly man. There is one person, Jesus Christ, with a divine and a human nature. Throughout church history, sceptics have sought to deny or limit the true deity of Jesus. Among those who want to revere Jesus, however, the tendency is to deny or at least downplay his true humanity. Yet it is essential that when Jesus was born by the virgin birth, the eternal Son of God took up a true human nature and became man. According to the Bible, in order for Jesus to pay the debt of man's sin, he must be a human being. The writer of Hebrews stated: 'he had to be made like his brothers in every respect... to make propitiation for the sins of the people' (*Heb.* 2:17).

In the early church, Gnostic philosophers taught that all matter is evil. Only spirit, they said, is noble and good. Under this view, it was inconceivable that God's Son truly suffered and died in a human body. Instead, they taught that Christ only seemed to be a man. This view is called *docetism*, for the Greek work *dokeo*, which means 'to seem'. While it seemed that the Christ was a man, he was instead a kind of phantom or, in an alternative view, the divine Spirit only temporarily occupied the human shell that was the man Jesus. In any case, though Christ seemed to be a man, he really was not.

It may have been with this heresy in mind that John records Jesus gasping, 'I thirst' (*John* 19:28). Charles Spurgeon writes: 'Jesus was proved to be really man, because he suffered the pains which belong to manhood. Angels cannot suffer thirst. A phantom, as some have called him, could not suffer in this fashion: but Jesus really suffered, not only the more refined pains of delicate and sensitive minds, but the rougher and commoner pangs of flesh and blood."[2]

Death by crucifixion inevitably involved the torment of extreme thirst. Jesus had suffered a great loss of fluids from his scourging and the shock to his entire system from the crucifixion would likely have caused a fever to wrack his body. Then hanging on a cross under the Near-Eastern sun, he felt the exquisite torture of severe dehydration.

John states that Jesus said, 'I thirst', 'knowing that all was now finished' (*John* 19:28). This statement indicates that Jesus was aware that his suffering of God's wrath had come to an end and it was now time for him to die. It is noteworthy that Jesus did not complain during earlier torments such as his two beatings by the Roman soldiers and the nailing of his body to the cross. Once the sixth hour came and Jesus began to suffer the infinite torment of God's wrath upon his spirit, it is likely that the comparatively lighter pains of his bodily torture were hardly noticed. But, now, Jesus' gasp, 'I thirst', indicates that the spiritual torment had concluded and the end of his sacrificial sufferings were before him.

John states as well that Jesus cried in thirst 'to fulfil the Scripture' (*John* 19:28). Commentators such as Donald Grey Barnhouse and A. W. Pink imagine that Jesus had been calmly perusing all the Old Testament prophecies of his death. Starting with Genesis, Jesus brought to mind all the detailed prophecies of the cross and made

---

[2] Charles H. Spurgeon, *Misery in Majesty*, 3 vols. (Edinburgh: Banner of Truth, 2005), 3:186-7.

sure before he died that all were fulfilled. When Jesus got to Psalm 69:21, he realized that its prophecy of his being forced to drink vinegar had not yet come to pass, so he said, 'I thirst', to provoke the soldiers to give him the sponge of sour wine to drink. This last prophecy having been fulfilled, Jesus was then free to die.

It may be true that Jesus spoke in part to prompt the soldiers to fulfil the ancient prophecy, but that interpretation does not seem to account for the pathos of Jesus' gasping words from the cross. John does not depict Jesus engaging in calm Bible scholarship, but rather shows Jesus suffering in the torment of his dying thirst. This episode fulfilled the Scripture, therefore, because Psalm 69 accurately foretold the physical and emotional suffering that Jesus endured in his crucifixion.[3]

Jesus' citation from Psalm 69 gives a commentary on his experience of suffering as he neared his death. David wrote this prayer for salvation when he was surrounded by enemies. The immediate context of Jesus' reference includes grief over the malice of his tormentors: 'Reproaches have broken my heart, so that I am in despair. I looked for pity, but there was none, and for comforters, but I found none. They gave me poison for food, and for my thirst they gave me sour wine to drink' (*Psa.* 69:20-21). Mark's Gospel confirms the lament of this psalm, combining both physical suffering and ridicule. When the ninth hour came at the end of Jesus' suffering, he cried aloud, 'My God, my God, why have you forsaken me?' Thinking he had called to Elijah, the on-looking soldiers gave Jesus their sour wine to keep him alive long enough to make fun of him (*Mark* 15:34-36). As John tells it: 'A jar full of sour wine stood there, so they put a sponge full of

---

[3] Taken this way, 'to fulfil the Scripture' refers to what comes before it rather than to Jesus' saying, 'I thirst.' The meaning would be that Jesus knew that 'all was now finished in order to fulfil the Scriptures', and then said, 'I thirst.' See J. C. Ryle, *John*, 3 vols. (Edinburgh, Banner of Truth, 1987), 3:359-60.

the sour wine on a hyssop branch and held it to his mouth. When Jesus had received the sour wine, he said, "It is finished", and he bowed his head and gave up his spirit' (*John* 19:29-30).

All through his account of the crucifixion, John has emphasized Jesus' sovereign mastery. It is therefore only at the end that Jesus bows his head, having apparently held it aloft throughout his torment. The expression 'bowed his head' is elsewhere used for the laying down of one's head on a pillow (*Matt.* 8:20), so that John sees Jesus peaceably placing his head into the Father's embrace. A normal crucifixion might continue for hours and sometimes even days. But, having endured the torment of God's wrath on the sins of his people, Jesus laid down his own life at the time of his own choosing. Matthew's Gospel tells us that so awesome and holy was the spectacle of Jesus yielding up his life that the centurion and the other soldiers supervising his cross exclaimed, 'Truly this was the Son of God!' (*Matt.* 27:54).

Hell Prefigured and Prevented

There are a number of things we should note about Jesus' cry of thirst and the response of the soldiers. First, we should realize the shocking irony of this event. John has noted many ironies throughout the account of Jesus' arrest, trial, and crucifixion. The greatest of these is the cry of thirst from the Saviour who is himself the fountain of life. Bruce Milne comments: 'So the one who offered living water, which would mean never thirsting again, the one who cried on the last day of the feast, "If anyone is thirsty, let him come to me and drink", he now cries, *I am thirsty*.'[4] Jesus suffered the bitter irony of this reversal not by some defect in himself, as if his own store of waters had run dry, but as a voluntary sacrifice on our behalf.

4 Bruce Milne, *The Message of John: Here Is Your King!* (Downers Grove, IL: Inter-Varsity, 1993), p. 281.

THE DEATH OF THE SAVIOUR

We can understand the significance of Jesus' suffering when we realize what a poignant picture of hell he presented when he cried, 'I thirst' (*John* 19:28). Sin often begins with a sensual appetite, as it did in the eating of fruit in the Garden, and it leads to an everlasting sensual torment. Part of the sufferings of hell will be 'the deprivation of every form of comfort. Man refused to obey his Creator—the time will come when the Creator will refuse to succor man.'[5]

We remember the parable Jesus taught about the tycoon who died and went to hell. The indulgent rich man had lived a selfish, greedy, and ungodly life and in death he went to the realms of torment. Burning with thirst in hell, he begged for godly Lazarus, a poor man he had neglected in life, to dip his finger in water and place just one cool drop on his tongue, for, he said, 'I am in anguish in this flame' (*Luke* 16:24). The request was denied because of the impassible gulf between heaven and hell and because God himself has ordained the eternal torment of all those who perish in their sins. Jesus, enduring our hell, experienced this same unabated, fiery thirst so that we would be saved from it. Charles Spurgeon wrote: 'if Jesus had not thirsted, every one of us would have thirsted for ever afar off from God, with an impassable gulf between us and heaven. Our sinful tongues, blistered by the fever of passion, must have burned for ever had not his tongue been tormented with thirst in our stead.'[6] Psalm 22:15 described the torment of thirst that Jesus endured as the penalty for our sin: 'my strength is dried up like a potsherd, and my tongue sticks to my jaws; you lay me in the dust of death.'

The response to Jesus' cry provides an accompanying portrait of the wickedness of man's sinful nature that deserves the torments

[5] Charles H. Spurgeon, *Metropolitan Tabernacle Pulpit*, 63 vols. (Pasedena, TX: Pilgrim Press, 1969), 59:758.
[6] Spurgeon, *Majesty in Misery*, 3:191.

of hell. We hear much today about the goodness and nobility of man, and for this reason people resent the Bible's teaching of sin and divine judgment. But look at noble mankind as God Incarnate cries for something to drink from the cross! When Jesus was to be born, man was unwilling to make room for him at the inn. Now as Jesus suffers the thirst of divine judgment, man has no soothing cup of water for him but shoves a vinegar-filled sponge into his bleeding mouth. The psalm that Jesus cites declares, 'I looked for pity, but there was none, and for comforters, but I found none... For my thirst they gave me sour wine to drink' (*Psa.* 69:20-21). The psalm goes on to plead for divine punishment on the cruelty of mankind: 'Add to them punishment upon punishment; may they have no acquittal from you. Let them be blotted out of the book of the living' (*Psa.* 69:27-28).

A final detail in this passage suggests Jesus' death as our only prevention from suffering the torments of hell. John writes that they put the sponge of sour wine 'on a hyssop branch and held it to his mouth' (*John* 19:29). Hyssop was a bush that produces a sponge-like blossom. Israel's priests used this plant for the brush with which to sprinkle the blood from the atoning sacrifices in the temple. David refers to it in Psalm 51:7: 'Purge me with hyssop, and I shall be clean; wash me, and I shall be whiter than snow.' Hyssop was also used during the first Passover in Egypt to daub the lambs' blood on the Israelite doorposts so the angel of death would pass over (*Exod.* 12:22). When the hyssop was lifted up to Jesus' mouth it was not to sprinkle blood for his cleansing, but for his blood to fall upon the hyssop, providing the true atoning blood to which David appealed when he sought to be cleansed of his sin.

Jesus' Death as Substitute and Sacrifice

John's record of Jesus' death points to the great reality that Jesus died as a substitute and sacrifice for sin. John recounts that Jesus 'knowing that all was now finished' (*John* 19:28), cried out in thirst, drank the sour wine, bowed down his head and 'gave up his spirit' (*John* 19:30). In foretelling this event, the prophet Isaiah made known its meaning: 'he was wounded for our transgressions; he was crushed for our iniquities; upon him was the chastisement that brought us peace, and with his stripes we are healed. All we like sheep have gone astray; we have turned—every one—to his own way; and the Lord has laid on him the iniquity of us all' (*Isa.* 53:5-6). The key ideas here are *substitute* and *sacrifice*. God sent his Son, Jesus, to die on the cross as a substitute for sinners, offering his life as sacrifice to pay the debt of sin for all who trust in his blood.

The background for these ideas is the penalty of death for breaking God's law. According to the Bible, 'None is righteous, no not one' (*Rom.* 3:10), since we have all sinned by breaking God's commands. We have all therefore come under the just condemnation of death; as Ezekiel 18:4 says, 'the soul who sins shall die'. The penalty of death for sin was taught to our first parents, Adam and Eve, at the beginning of the Bible. God commanded them to obey under the threat of death (*Gen.* 2:16-17), which included both physical and spiritual death. Adam broke God's command and as our covenant head he thereby cast our whole race into sin (see *Rom.* 5:12-14). For this reason, and since we have all confirmed our condemnation by committing our own personal sins, we are all justly condemned to suffer both the physical death of our bodies and the everlasting death of our souls in hell. It was to save us from this penalty that the God of grace sent his Son Jesus to die in the place of his people. We deserve death as the consequence of our sins, but Jesus substituted himself in our place on the cross and offered himself as a sacrifice to satisfy God's law against the debt of our sin.

One of the best illustrations of Jesus' death as a substitute and sacrifice is the one God provided to Adam and Eve after they had sinned in the Garden. God had threatened disobedience with death, saying, 'of the tree of the knowledge of good and evil you shall not eat, for in the day that you eat of it you shall surely die' (*Gen.* 2:17). But after sinning Adam and Eve had not suffered their punishment. How would God's justice be served if Adam and Eve did not die for their sin? Genesis 3:21 answers that 'the LORD God made for Adam and for his wife garments of skins and clothed them.'

Imagine the dreadful wonder of our first parents, who had never envisioned the death of one of God's creatures. God caused a substitute to die in Adam and Eve's place, the first death that anyone had ever seen! The sinless animals died as a sacrifice to pay the debt of their sin and then they were covered in the sinless skins of the sacrificed animals. 'So this is death!' Adam and Eve must have cried in horror. James Boice comments: 'Yet even as they recoiled from the sacrifice, they must have marveled as well, for what God was showing was that although they themselves deserved to die it was possible for another, in this case two animals, to die in their place.'[7]

Adam and Eve would have realized that the death of animals could never take away the stain of human sin. The writer of Hebrews stated that the animal sacrifices of the Old Testament were never understood actually to atone for human sin, but were a constant reminder of sin and of the need for a true atonement, since 'it is impossible for the blood of bulls and goats to take away sins' (*Heb.* 10:4). This is why John the Baptist spoke as the last prophet of the Old Testament, pointing to Jesus as the true substitute for sinners and the true sacrifice for sin: 'Behold, the Lamb of God, who takes away the sin of the world' (*John* 1:29). Jesus died as a substitute and sacrifice for those who confess their sins to God and look to Jesus in faith for salvation. John 3:16 says, 'For God so loved the world,

[7] James Montgomery Boice, *The Gospel of John*, 5 vols. (Grand Rapids, MI: Baker, 1999), 5:1527.

that he gave his only Son, that whoever believes in him should not perish but have eternal life.'

This reminds us that when Jesus laid down his head upon the bosom of the Father and 'gave up his spirit', he did not die as a victim but as a victor. 'It is finished', he cried at the end, having completed the sacrifice that pays the debt of our sin in the courts of God's holy justice (*John* 19:30).

Hymns abound that sentimentalize the sacrificial death of Jesus for his people. Bernard of Clairvaux sang,

> What language shall I borrow to thank thee, dearest Friend,
> For this, thy dying sorrow, thy pity without end?
> O make me thine forever; and should I fainting be
> Lord, let me never, never outlive my love to thee.[8]

The sacrifice of Christ is worthy of all such admiration and love. But we must be sure to do more than admire the sacrifice of Jesus on the cross. We first must sing,

> Bearing shame and scoffing rude,
> In my place condemned He stood
> Sealed my pardon with his blood:
> Hallelujah! what a Saviour![9]

To be saved we must personally take our own sins to the cross, confessing them to God and entrusting them to Christ our Saviour, that he would bear them as our substitute and offer himself as our sacrifice to satisfy God's just wrath.

Jesus' Thirst for Salvation

Preachers of this text have long seen one last sense in Jesus' cry, 'I thirst.' Spurgeon writes:

[8] Bernard of Clairvaux (1091-1153), 'O Sacred Head, Now Wounded', 1153.
[9] Philip P. Bliss (1838-1876), 'Man of Sorrows! What a Name', 1875.

Christ is always thirsting after the salvation of precious souls, and that cry on the cross... was the outburst of the great heart of Jesus Christ as he saw the multitude and he cried unto his God, 'I thirst.' He thirsted to redeem mankind, he thirsted to accomplish the work of our salvation. This very day he thirsteth still in that respect, as he is still willing to receive those that come to him, still resolved that such as come shall never be cast out, and still desires that they may come.[10]

Whether or not this interpretation accurately assesses Jesus' cry of thirst from the cross, it certainly fits Jesus' constant burden for the salvation of others who are dying in sin. Jesus cried, 'I thirst', so that we may never thirst; he died that we might have eternal life. Once at the feast, Jesus called out, 'If anyone thirsts, let him come to me and drink' (*John* 7:37). Jesus told the woman of Samaria, 'whoever drinks of the water that I will give him will never be thirsty forever' (*John* 4:14). Therefore, through faith in him our souls are filled with the life of God that Jesus sends by the Holy Spirit. To drink from the troughs of this world—the fountain of sinful pleasure, the well of pride, the pool of worldly attainment – is to be ever thirsty, never satisfied and always left to cry, 'I thirst.' But with the cup of simple faith we may drink and be filled from Christ's river of life: 'I came that they may have life', Jesus said, 'and have it abundantly' (*John* 10:10).

According to the Bible, there are only two thirsts that Jesus would have his people continue to feel. The first is the inner longing for more of him in our hearts. Jesus would have our souls be yet thirsty until he is our all in this life and our glory in the life to come. The psalmist sang, 'As a deer pants for flowing streams, so pants my soul for you, O God. My soul thirsts for God, for the living God' (*Psa.* 42:1-2). This is a thirst that will be filled: since Jesus took the wrathful cup of sour wine to his thirsty lips,

---

[10] Spurgeon, *Metropolitan Tabernacle Pulpit*, 59:759.

believers may look for the cup of fellowship with God to be placed onto ours.

The second thirst that Jesus would have us to know is his own thirst for the saving of souls. He would have parents shed such tears for the salvation of their children that they rise up from prayer with a hunger and thirst after righteousness (*Matt.* 5:6). As Jesus once stopped for a drink at the well in Samaria (*John* 4:6-7), he would likewise have us know the thirst of weariness in our labours for the salvation of friends, family members, and even those far away in distant lands. The Saviour who thirsted on the cross now beckons all who will come to drink from the life that he gives, and then bids us to share the invitation with others. In fact, it is with his invitation to drink that Jesus speaks for the last time in all the Bible: 'The Spirit and the bride say, "Come!" And let him who hears say, "Come!" Whoever is thirsty, let him come; and whoever wishes, let him take the free gift of the water of life' (*Rev.* 22:17, NIV).

4

WHY DID JESUS DIE?
John 19:30

When Jesus had received the sour wine, he said, 'It is finished,' and he bowed his head and gave up his spirit (*John* 19:30).

IN the eleventh century A.D., Anselm of Canterbury (1033-1109) published one of the most significant theology books ever written, a work that significantly aided the understanding of Christians on a vitally important doctrinal matter. The book was titled *Cur Deus Homo*, which in English means 'Why the God-Man' or 'Why God Became Man'. The book arose from conversations Anselm had with a man named Boso, who was one of many people during that time who sought to be enlightened in the gospel. Responding to this earnest spiritual hunger for truth, Anselm applied his keen mind to the Bible's teaching of the incarnation and atonement of Christ. Later, Anselm published his conclusions, thinking them important for the good of the wider church.

Of all the important topics presented in *Cur Deus Homo*, probably the most significant was Anselm's teaching on the purpose and design of Christ's death. Up until his time, the leading theory of the atonement in the Western church was the ransom theory. This teaching followed Jesus' important statement that 'the Son of Man came… to give his life as a ransom for many' (*Matt.* 20:28). As the early church conceived this ransom, Christ died to offer a payment in his blood to the Devil, who held mankind captive in sin. Even so great a theologian as Augustine of Hippo spoke of the cross as 'the Devil's mousetrap.'[1] Under this view, Satan had secured the right of possession over mankind because of sin, so that Christ had to offer his death to the Devil. Satan thought he had secured his victory over Jesus, but the power of divine life that he 'swallowed' at the cross overthrew his realm of evil and death.

Anselm correctly saw that this ransom theory gave too much credit to Satan, who never possessed a true right to mankind. Man's true debt is to God's holy justice and honour; it was the broken law, not Satan, that held sinful man in condemnation. This insight reveals man's predicament in sin. Anselm observed: 'Sinful man owes God a debt for sin which he cannot repay, and at the same time he cannot be saved without repaying.'[2] This problem, unsolvable from the position of the sinner, who possesses no coin with which to pay his debt of sin, provides the answer to the mystery of why God became man. It also answers a question raised by Jesus' cry from the cross. Hearing Jesus' victory peal, 'It is finished' (*John* 19:30), we ask, 'Why did Jesus die?'

Theories of the Atonement
Like all great theologians, Anselm was immediately opposed and severely criticized for his work. His chief opponent was his former student, the French theologian Peter Abelard (1079-1142). Abelard argued that Christ did not die to make any payment at all, but merely offered himself as an example of divine love and human virtue. This theory is called the 'subjective' theory of the atonement, since it grounds the purpose of the cross in the subjective experience of the Bible reader rather than in any objective achievement of Jesus'

---

[1] Quoted from Stephen J. Nichols, *Pages from Church History: A Guided Tour of Christian Classics* (Phillipsburg, NJ: P&R, 2006), p. 101.
[2] Nichols, *Pages*, pp. 103-4.

death. Philip Ryken explains that in this approach, 'The death of Christ was not satisfactory, in the sense of providing atonement for sin, but exemplary, in the sense of showing the way to suffer and die with courage.' Although Abelard's teaching was denounced as heresy in 1121, his theory of Christ's death is standard teaching in liberal churches today. Ryken comments, 'Whenever we hear Jesus presented more as an example than as a Saviour, we are hearing the sons and daughters of Abelard.'[3]

In terms of his medieval context, Anselm's satisfaction theory of the atonement emphasized sinful man's insult to God's *honour*. Later theologians added to this the Bible's emphasis on sin's violation of God's *justice*. The biblical description of sin as transgression, for instance, means a violation of God's law, to which God responds with just wrath. James states that one who fails to keep God's law is accountable to divine justice, having 'become a transgressor of the law' (2:11). Realizing this, evangelical Christians have emphasized that Jesus died to pay the penalty for the transgressions of his people. This view is called *penal substitutionary atonement*, meaning that Jesus atoned for our sins by bearing their penalty as our substitute before God's unyielding justice.

Opponents have long derided this view of the cross. Episcopal bishop John Shelby Spong wrote, 'I would choose to loathe rather than to worship a deity who required the sacrifice of his son.'[4] This opinion was not surprising coming from a humanist who denies the Bible. But more recently, similar attacks have arisen from within evangelical ranks. British writer Steve Chalke described the classic evangelical doctrine of the atonement as 'a form of cosmic child abuse – a vengeful Father, punishing his Son for an offence he has

[3] Philip G. Ryken, 'The Medieval Achievement: Anselm on the Atonement', in Richard D. Phillips, ed., *Precious Blood: The Atoning Work of Christ* (Wheaton, IL: Crossway, 2009), p. 138.
[4] John Shelby Spong, *Why Christianity Must Change or Die* (San Francisco, CA: HarperCollins, 1999), p. 95.

not even committed.'[5] Joel B. Green and Mark D. Baker wrote that in the traditional evangelical doctrine of the cross 'God takes on the role of the sadist inflicting punishment, while Jesus, in his role as masochist, readily embraces suffering.'[6] These and similar assaults on the idea of Jesus dying for our sins are issued in books printed by publishing houses long associated with evangelical Christianity.

In the place of penal substitutionary atonement, critics would have us embrace the liberal subjective view of the atonement or an updated version of the pre-Anselm ransom view known as the *Christus Victor* theory. *Christus Victor* asserts that Jesus died to overthrow the cosmic powers of darkness. This is undoubtedly true, but the question remains as to *how* Jesus overthrew the power of Satan, evil, and death. The Bible's answer is that since 'the sting of death is sin, and the power of sin is the law' (*1 Cor.* 15:56), Christ overthrew these powers by satisfying God's law. Jesus accomplished this through both his own perfect lifelong obedience and his death as our substitute before the law's penalty for sin.

John tells us that before Jesus died, he cried out, 'It is finished' (*John* 19:30), referring to a definite work he had achieved. Peter identified this finished work by referring to penal substitutionary atonement: 'he himself bore our sins in his body on the tree' (*1 Pet.* 2:24). To hang on a tree was to bear God's curse (*Deut.* 21:23); Jesus died under this judgment because he 'bore our sins.' Paul went so far as to describe as 'of first importance' the teaching that 'Christ died for our sins in accordance with the Scriptures' (*1 Cor.* 15:3). In light of these definitive biblical statements, we see that while there are many facets of Christ's atonement, including

---

[5] Steve Chalke, *The Lost Message of Jesus* (Grand Rapids, MI: Zondervan, 2003), p. 182.

[6] Joel B. Green and Mark D. Baker, *Recovering the Scandal of the Cross: Atonement in New Testament and Contemporary Contexts* (Downers Grove, IL: InterVarsity Press, 2000), p. 30.

Christ's victory over evil and his display of divine love, the key to them all is penal substitutionary atonement.

The Accomplishment of the Atonement

Another way to answer the question 'Why did Jesus die?' is to consider what Christ accomplished on the cross. Penal substitutionary atonement tells us what Jesus did: he died to pay the penalty for our sins. But when Jesus cried out, 'It is finished,' what was the result and achievement of that payment? The answer is found in three words that every Christian should know and understand: propitiation, redemption, and reconciliation.

Propitiation is a concept that comes from the temple and the Old Testament sacrificial system. The Bible teaches that God's wrath burns against all sin, so in saving his people Jesus died to assuage God's wrath against the sinner. This teaching is classically stated in Romans 3:25, where Paul writes that 'God put [Christ] forward as a propitiation by his blood, to be received by faith.' Man's problem is stated in Romans 3:23: 'all have sinned and fall short of the glory of God.' Sinners can still, however, be 'justified by [God's] grace as a gift, through the redemption that is in Christ Jesus' (*Rom.* 3:24). How can this happen? On what basis are sinners redeemed from sin and justified before God? Paul's answer is that God set forward his Son Jesus to die as a sacrifice to pacify his wrath towards our sin.

The Greek word for propitiation is *hilasterion,* which translates the Hebrew word for the *mercy seat* that sat atop the ark of the covenant in the Holy of Holies, the inner sanctum of God's temple where his glory dwelt. Here, sacrificial blood was spread once a year for the sins of the people on the Day of Atonement. The high priest came before the throne of God, where two golden cherubim gazed down upon the tablets of God's broken law. The priest then poured the blood on the mercy seat atop the ark, averting God's wrath, since God now saw not the broken law but the sacrificial blood. Paul says that Jesus Christ was that sacrifice, his the true blood of the mercy seat that propitiates God's wrath so that sinners may be accepted by God.

Some critics recoil at the idea of propitiation, considering it morally objectionable for God to require a sacrifice in order to forgive and pointing out the similarity of this doctrine with pagan rites of human sacrifice. The answer to this objection is that the pagan rites arose from a true recognition of man's need for a substitute to die for sin. The ancient Mayans, for instance, sacrificed vast thousands of lives in a quest for atonement. They failed to realize, however, that no multitude of sinful humans can offer an acceptable sacrifice to propitiate God's wrath; since each sinner receives his own punishment, he cannot die for others.[7] This is why Christianity does *not* teach that sinners must make a sacrifice to avert God's wrath, but rather that God himself provided the sacrifice to avert his wrath against our sin. God sent his Son, the God-man Jesus Christ, to offer his infinitely precious life as the propitiation for our sins.

The last word in the Bible on propitiation – literally, its last reference – is given by the apostle John. In 1 John 4:10, the beloved disciple turns the complaints about propitiation onto their heads. What does it say about such a God, people bemoan, if he requires a sacrifice before he is willing to forgive? John replies, 'In this is love, not that we have loved God but that he loved us and sent his Son to be the propitiation for our sins' (*1 John* 4:10). When we did not love God, he loved us by sending Jesus, his Son, to be the sacrifice for our sin. The biblical doctrine of propitiation, therefore, declares God's saving love for sinners.

The second great term for what Jesus accomplished on the cross is *redemption*. This is a term borrowed from the market-place,

[7] See Wendy Murray Zoba, 'Maya Mysteries' in *Books & Culture*, vol. 8, no. 1 (Jan/Feb 2002), p. 28.

involving the making of a purchase. Redemption presupposes some kind of bondage or captivity, circumstances that afflict us but from which we are not able to free ourselves. Redemption takes us from slavery to freedom, and from affliction to salvation. The greatest Old Testament example of redemption was God's deliverance of Israel from their bondage in Egypt in the exodus. God told Moses: 'I will free you from being slaves to them, and I will redeem you with an outstretched arm and with mighty acts of judgment' (*Exod.* 6:6-7).

Redemption, therefore, speaks of God saving us from a situation we could never get ourselves out of, just as the Israelites would have remained in Egypt forever if God had not come to their aid. The New Testament takes this concept and applies it to the problem of our sin, which we could never solve by ourselves. We think of sins as a small matter, indulgences that do us little harm, but the Bible says that sin results in slavery and crushing misery out of which we are totally unable to escape on our own.

In the ancient world, there were three ways you could become a slave, and all three of them relate to our bondage to sin. First, a person might be born into slavery, and in the same way the Bible says that since Adam's fall, we all are born into sin, inheriting from Adam a corrupted nature. David thus lamented: 'Surely I was sinful at birth, sinful from the time my mother conceived me' (*Psa.* 51:5). Second, a person might be enslaved as a result of military defeat. Likewise, we are mastered by sin's power over our flesh and overcome by temptations. Third, one might have debts he could not pay and thus be sold into slavery. Similarly, our sin creates a debt before God's justice that we can never repay. In all of these ways, our situation in sin is like that of a slave. Slaves lead lives of misery and bondage, and these are the very things that sin does to us.

That is the bad news of our sin, as Jesus declared, 'Everyone who sins is a slave to sin' (*John* 8:34). The good news of the gospel answers this predicament. Paul writes, 'In [Christ] we have redemption through his blood, the forgiveness of our trespasses' (*Eph.* 1:7).

Perhaps the greatest Bible story teaching redemption is that of the prophet Hosea and his marriage to the sinful woman Gomer. Gomer faithlessly abandoned Hosea and pursued her many lovers, descending further and further into sin. All the while, God commanded Hosea to remain faithful to her, as a picture of his faithfulness to sinful Israel. Ultimately, Gomer's sin caused her to be sold on the auction block as a slave, probably to pay debts she had incurred. Slaves were typically sold in the town square, stripped naked for all to inspect. This pictures the degradation into which sin seeks to drag us all.

The men gathered to place bids on the body of this female slave. 'Twelve pieces of silver,' bid one. 'Thirteen,' called a voice from the back that Gomer may no longer have recognized. 'Fourteen,' came the reply. 'Fifteen,' said Hosea. 'Fifteen silver pieces and a bushel of barley,' came the counter bid. Stepping forward and reaching out to his wife, Hosea spoke, 'Fifteen pieces of silver and a bushel and a half of barley.' Everyone realized he could not be outbid and so the other men began to walk away. Gomer was rightly his already, but sin had torn her away. Now Hosea had bought her back with everything he had and draped her with his love: 'So I bought her for fifteen shekels of silver and about a homer and a lethek of barley. Then I told her, "You are to live with me many days; you must not be a prostitute or be intimate with any man, and I will live with you"' (*Hos.* 3:2-3).

If we are in Christ, this is our story as well. James Boice comments:

> We were created for intimate fellowship with God and for freedom, but we have disgraced ourselves by unfaithfulness. First we have flirted with and then committed adultery with this sinful world and its values. The world even bid for our soul, offering sex, money,

fame, power and all the other items in which it traffics. But Jesus, our faithful bridegroom and lover, entered the market place to buy us back. He bid his own blood. There is no higher bid than that. And we became his. He reclothed us, not in the wretched rags of our old unrighteousness, but in his new robes of righteousness. He has said to us, 'You must dwell as mine… you shall not belong to another… so will I also be to you.'[8]

When Jesus cried, 'It is finished,' the final term for understanding his achievement is *reconciliation*. This idea comes from the realm of the family: we are reconciled to the Father's love through the blood of Christ.

Reconciliation assumes that by sin we were, as Paul writes, 'alienated from the life of God' (*Eph.* 4:18). The good news of the cross is that God has reconciled us to himself through the blood of Christ, making peace with those who were at war with his rule. We must never think that Jesus died to reconcile us to an otherwise unwilling Father. Rather, Paul insists, 'All this is from God, who through Christ reconciled us to himself' (*2 Cor.* 5:18). Paul explains how God accomplished this reconciliation in one of the Bible's great verses: 'For our sake [God] made him to be sin who knew no sin, so that in him we might become the righteousness of God' (*2 Cor.* 5:21). God imputed our sin to Christ and Christ's perfect righteousness to us, so that we might be clothed in pure white to draw near to his holy love.

It was with these achievements in his triumphant heart that Jesus cried out, 'It is finished' (*John* 19:30). Sin had ruined God's relationship with man, but Jesus overcame this barrier by propitiating God's wrath against our sin. The cross also delivered Christ's people from sin's power, redeeming us to salvation freedom

---

[8] James Montgomery Boice, *Foundations of the Christian Faith* (Downers Grove, IL: InterVarsity, 1986), pp. 329-30.

with the coin of his blood. Having satisfied wrath on God's part and overthrown captivity on our part, Christ now grants sinners reconciliation with God through faith in his blood. Paul explained: 'you, who once were alienated and hostile in mind, doing evil deeds, he has now reconciled in his body of flesh by his death, in order to present you holy and blameless and above reproach before him' (*Col.* 1:21-22).

The Necessity of the Atonement

Why did Jesus die? We have answered by identifying Christ's death as a penal substitutionary atonement and by recognizing his achievement on the cross in terms of propitiation, redemption, and reconciliation. This leaves one important question about Jesus' death: why did Jesus *have* to die? Was the atonement truly necessary?

There are three ways in which we might answer this question. The first answer is to say that it was not necessary for God to send his Son to die on the cross. God was not in any way obliged to save the sinful creatures who had rebelled against his rule. Man has no right to demand salvation and no one could quarrel if God subjected us all to eternal punishment for our sins. The only necessity of salvation arises from God's own character. It is true that God's holy nature burns in just anger against all sin (*Rom.* 1:18). But it is also true that God's loving nature delights in mercy (*Mic.* 7:18). This loving mercy within God provided a necessity for salvation within himself: God's grace alone accounts for God ordaining to save a great company of people out of the human race (*Rom.* 9:15-16).

Since God's nature moves him to save his people, we then ask if Christ's death was the necessary way for this to be achieved. Some have answered that the cross was not absolutely necessary and that there may have been other ways for God to save. Thomas Aquinas argued this view by stating that the atonement was only contingently necessary. He meant that God might have saved his people by some other means, but once God chose to save by Christ's incarnation and atonement then Jesus' death became necessary. While there were other possible ways in which a holy God could save sinners, this was the way God chose as most advantageous to his own glory.

The problem with this view is that it is inconceivable that God should have required the sacrificial death of his Son had there been any other way to redeem his people from sin. The cross was therefore not relatively or contingently necessary for our salvation, but as John Gerstner has put it, 'the atonement must be antecedently, absolutely necessary, for there was no other way it could have been done... It had to be and it was absolutely necessary that [Jesus] should take our nature upon himself. In that nature, the Lord Jesus Christ made a true, infinite, and satisfactory expiation of our guilt in the atonement in which we glory.'[9]

Once man had fallen into sin, the problem of salvation involved the justification of those who deserve punishment. How can God uphold his perfect justice, remaining unstained in his holiness, and at the same time extend his mercy in a loving salvation of sinners? God's answer – the only possible answer – is that another must suffer the judgment in the place of those who are condemned. This raises the question: Who can offer this sacrifice? Who is both willing and able to die for sinners under God's wrath?

This was the question for which Anselm offered the Bible's answer in *Cur Deus Homo*. He pointed out that no sinner could offer the sacrifice, since a sinner already owed his life to pay for his own sins. Moreover, sin has so affected all mankind that we cannot even choose to please God and thus cannot offer a true offering.

---

[9] John R. Gerstner, 'The Atonement and the Purpose of God', in Gabriel N. E. Fluhrer, ed., *Atonement* (Phillipsburg, NJ: P&R, 2010), p. 62. See Gerstner's discussion of this issue on pages 61-63.

Therefore, Anselm reasoned that only God himself possessed the moral purity and divine life to offer the needed sacrifice for sin. This posed another problem, since it is man who owes the debt to God's justice and therefore man who must make the sacrifice to pay for sin. The resolution of this problem was the final answer to the title of Anselm's book, 'Why God Became Man'. He wrote:

> the debt was so great that, while man alone owed it, only God could pay it, so that the same person must be both man and God. Thus it was necessary for God to take manhood into the unity of his Person, so that he who in his own nature ought to pay and could not should be in a person who could... The life of this one man was so sublime, so precious, that it can suffice to pay what is owing for the sins of the whole world, and infinitely more.[10]

Jesus' death for sin was absolutely necessary, since there was no other way for God to be both 'just and the justifier of the one who has faith in Jesus' (*Rom.* 3:26). This is the necessity of which Jesus spoke to Nicodemus earlier in John's Gospel: 'so must the Son of Man be lifted up, that whoever believes in him may have eternal life' (*John* 3:14-15).

The Exceeding Gravity of Sin

This leaves only one question: do you accept the necessity of Jesus' death for your salvation? Do you confess that only if God's Son should have paid the debt of your sin can you be saved from the holy justice of God? This is a necessity that many people reject. Some claim that they will make their own way to salvation. Others object to the idea that there is only one way to heaven and insist that many other roads lead to God. The Christian answer to these objections is one given by Anselm when addressing the same

---

[10] Eugene R. Fairwether, ed., *A Scholastic Miscellany: Anselm to Ockham*, 'The Library of Christian Classics,' vol. 10 (Philadelphia, PA: Westminster, 1956), p. 176.

matter over nine hundred years ago. Replying to those who denied the need for an atonement to make satisfaction for man's guilt, Anselm wrote: 'You have not yet considered the exceeding gravity of sin.'[11] Sin is a personal affront to God's holy honour, and it must receive his personal, burning wrath. Sin is a rebellious transgression of God's law, and it must be punished for God's perfect justice to stand. So exceedingly great is the gravity of sin that you owe God for your sins a debt which you cannot repay, and at the same time you cannot be saved unless that debt is paid. God's gracious provision, his saving gift to you, is the atoning death of Christ which he now calls you to receive in faith, giving yourself to the Saviour who gave himself for you.

The world yet insists that all roads lead to God, and the world is right. Of course all roads to lead to God, for God is the alpha and omega of all things. But the horror that unbelievers will discover, if God's Word is true, is that the God to whom they arrive by any other way than the cross of Christ is an angry, offended, and awesomely holy God, whose perfect justice must consign them to an eternity of punishment in divine wrath. Yet the cross of Christ still stands before rebel mankind, pleading atoning mercy for all who will come to God by the one way of his Redeemer Son.

Jesus died to propitiate God's holy wrath, redeem believers from the guilt and power of sin, and reconcile all who will come to the adoring love of the Father. If you will come, then you will have a new answer for Anselm's question, 'Why did God become man?' and also to the question raised by the cross, 'Why did Jesus die?' You will answer, on the authority of God's Word: 'Jesus became man and died for me, that I might be forgiven, redeemed from my sin, and together with all of Christ's people belong to him and enjoy God's love forever.'

[11] Ryken, 'The Medieval Achievement', p. 134.

5

FINISHED!
John 19:30

'It is finished' (*John* 19:30).

M Y father had an expressive sense of humour that was often conveyed through his use of different languages. To express a sense of urgency, he would usually turn to the German language. He would bark out 'Schnell!' for 'quickly' and 'verstehen sie?' to ask 'do you understand?' with a tone of command. For more joyful expressions, my dad would move to Spanish or Italian. I especially remember his joyful cry when a difficult project or unpleasant chore was finished. 'Fini!' he would cry, or 'Finito!'

John tells us that when Jesus had completed his atoning work on the cross, before he gave up his spirit to the Father he also cried out, 'It is finished' (*John* 19:30). We do not know the tone of voice in which Jesus spoke this word (it is a single word in both Greek and Aramaic). It is hard to imagine, after all Jesus had gone through, that he spoke without a tone of exhaustion or pain. Yet it is certain that, as Leon Morris writes: 'Jesus died with the cry of the Victor on his lips. This is not the moan of the defeated, nor the sigh of patient resignation. It is the triumphant recognition that he has now fully accomplished the work that he came to do.'[1] For all

[1] Leon Morris, *The Gospel According to John* (Revised), New International Commentary on the New Testament (Grand Rapids, MI: Eerdmans, 1995), p. 720.

who read John's Gospel with faith in Jesus' saving work, his cry, 'It is finished', is therefore a source of pure joy and spiritual blessing in any language.

Christ's Finished Work

Although the Greek for 'It is finished' is only one word, that word expresses more than what comes through in the English translation. Charles Spurgeon stated, 'It would need all the other words that were ever spoken, or ever can be spoken, to explain this one word. It is altogether immeasurable. It is high; I cannot attain to it. It is deep; I cannot fathom it.'[2] There are important things we can say, however, about the Greek word *tetelestai*, which means, 'It is finished'. This word means more than that something has been completed. D. A. Carson comments, 'The verb *teleo* from which this form derives denotes the carrying out of a task, and in religious contexts bears the overtone of fulfilling one's religious obligations.'[3] This word, in other forms, has appeared repeatedly during the final days of Jesus' ministry. In his farewell prayer on the previous evening, Jesus anticipated this moment, saying to the Father, 'I glorified you on earth, having *accomplished* the work that you gave me to do' (*John* 17:4, italics mine, Greek, *teleiosas*). The apostle John wrote of Jesus' ministry earlier that evening: 'having loved his own who were in the world, he loved them *to the end*' (*John* 13:1, italics mine, Greek, *eis telos*). In this same vein, Jesus now announces the completion of his task on the cross, 'It is finished'.

As Jesus prepared to deliver his spirit into the Father's hands, what did he envision having been completed and accomplished? First, he had completed the sufferings necessary to his atoning death for our sins. We know that this was at least part of Jesus'

---

[2] C. H. Spurgeon, *Sermons on the Gospel of John* (Grand Rapids, MI: Zondervan, 1966), p. 170.

[3] D. A. Carson, *The Gospel of John* (Grand Rapids, MI: Eerdmans, 1991), p. 621.

meaning, since his cry cites the conclusion of Psalm 22, an Old Testament passage that chronicles his sufferings on the cross. No more would Jesus experience the terrible pain of scourging and crucifixion, endure the mocking ridicule of Roman soldiers and Jewish priests, and, worst of all, suffer the agony of divine wrath and separation from God's love. Mark Johnson comments on the sheer joy that must filled Jesus' heart as he spoke his last and dying words: 'Father, into your hands I commit my spirit!' (*Luke* 23:46): 'The only moment he had ever known when he could not call God 'Father' was over, and even as he prepares for death he is able... to take once more that term of intimate communion upon his lips' (*Luke* 23:46).'[4] How glad we are that Jesus' sufferings are finished and man's fury can never score him again!

> The head that once was crowned with thorns
> Is crowned with glory now:
> A royal diadem adorns
> The mighty Victor's brow.[5]

Second, Jesus had now fulfilled all the prophecies of his life and death. How thorough the prophetic preview had been of what Jesus would endure for our sins! Virtually every important detail in the tragedy of Christ's cross was publicized in advance. His betrayal by a friend (*Psa.* 41:9), the disciples forsaking him (*Psa.* 31:11), the false accusations and Jesus' silence before the judges (*Psa.* 35:11; *Isa.* 53:7), his formal acquittal (*Isa.* 53:9), his being numbered with transgressors (*Isa.* 53:12), his crucifixion (*Psa.* 22:16), the mocking of the on-lookers (*Psa.* 109:25), the taunt about his failure to save himself (*Psa.* 22:7-8), the soldiers' gambling for his clothing (*Psa.* 22:18), his prayer for his enemies (*Isa.* 53:12), his being forsaken of God (*Psa.* 22:1), his thirsting cry (*Psa.* 69:21), his yielding up

---

[4] Mark Johnson, *Let's Study John* (Edinburgh: Banner of Truth, 2003), p. 248.
[5] Thomas Kelly (1769-1855), 'The Head that Once Was Crowned', 1820.

of his spirit into the Father's hands (*Psa.* 31:5), the preservation of his bones from being broken (*Psa.* 34:20), and his burial in a rich man's tomb (*Isa.* 53:9) were all foretold in the prophetic witness. What an awe-inspiring proof of the divine inspiration of Scripture we have in the prophecies of Jesus' death!

> How firm a foundation ye saints of the Lord,
> is laid for your faith in His excellent Word![6]

If there ever is to be a Messiah who fulfils the legions of prophecies given to authenticate his life and death, that Messiah could only be Jesus Christ, who fulfilled them all in a way that no one else could ever do.

Most importantly, we see in Jesus' cry the declaration of his finished work for our salvation. John Calvin observes that Jesus' cry from the cross points out the centrality of the atonement to the Christian faith, since it 'shows that the whole accomplishment of our salvation, and all the parts of it, are contained in his death.'[7] Mark Johnson adds, 'His shout of accomplishment was the cry for which creation had been waiting since the fall of Adam.'[8]

Earlier in his ministry, Jesus taught, 'the Son of Man came not to be served but to serve, and to give his life as a ransom for many' (*Matt.* 20:28). That ransom payment had now been made and redemption had been achieved for the people who belong to Christ. There now remained nothing for Jesus to do in terms of his atoning work of satisfying God's wrath and redeeming his people from the bondage of sin. God the Son had been born of the virgin, had taken up a human nature, had lived a perfect life, and now had died a sacrificial death. All this was now accomplished! Jesus had

[6] Rippon's *Selection of Hymns*, 'How Firm a Foundation', 1787.
[7] John Calvin, *Calvin's Commentaries*, 23 vols. (Grand Rapids, MI: Baker, 1848, reprint 2009), 18:234.
[8] Johnson, *Let's Study John*, p. 248.

said, 'I am the good shepherd. The good shepherd lays down his life for the sheep' (*John* 10:11). That promise had been fulfilled and Christ's sheep had now been saved by his blood. He came to do it, he had said he would do it, and now Jesus had finished his saving work perfectly.

When Christians say that they have faith in Jesus Christ, we mean that we are relying on the finished work that he completed on the cross. Joseph Ryan writes: 'When Buddha died, it is reported by tradition that his last words were, "Strive without ceasing." Jesus' last words were, "I have done it." Religion tells us to finish the work—to go out and do something and be something. Jesus says, "Receive the finished work."'[9]

Resting in what Jesus has done, we need never fear the punishment of our sins, nor worry that God's law will condemn us in the end. We may rest on what he has completed, knowing that all that needed to be done for us to be saved has been done, finished on the cross.

Many Christians live in needless loathing before God, thinking themselves unacceptable and despised because of their sinfulness and failure, when the truth is that Jesus has finished removing the whole of sin as an obstacle to our acceptance with God. With joy we may now take up Paul's challenge in Romans 8:34: 'Who is to condemn? Christ Jesus is the one who died— more than that, who was raised—who is at the right hand of God, who indeed is interceding for us.' Looking at our own works we see everything as not only unfinished and imperfect, but as positively damning. But looking at Jesus' dying work on the cross, we know that our salvation is finished by a perfect offering of the once-for-all sacrifice that truly frees us from our sin.

[9] Joseph 'Skip' Ryan, *That You May Believe* (Wheaton, IL: Crossway, 2003), p. 342.

THE DEATH OF THE SAVIOUR

Paid in Full

One way fully to appreciate the saving significance of Jesus' cry, 'It is finished,' is to see that the Greek word *tetelestai* was used in commercial transactions to signify that a debt was paid in full. The word would be stamped on a purchase or written on a receipt to show that no more payment was needed and the purchase was complete. When Jesus spoke this word, he was declaring that he had now paid every last penny of his people's sin-debt to God's justice and that our redemption had been fully and eternally accomplished. This is why Peter wrote to the early Christians that 'you were ransomed from the futile ways inherited from your forefathers, not with perishable things such as silver or gold, but with the precious blood of Christ, like that of a lamb without blemish or spot' (*1 Pet.* 1:18-19).

Another place we see this same truth regarding Jesus' finished sacrifice is Hebrews 1:3. The writer of Hebrews set forth the supremacy of Christ's ministry by writing: 'After making purification for sins, he sat down at the right hand of the Majesty on high'. Priests in the Old Testament never sat down in the temple, for there was no place for them to sit. The reason was that they were offering only a temporary sacrifice; there would always be more blood to be shed so their work was never done. But when Jesus had offered his own blood for our sins, he sat down on his royal throne, for there were no more priestly sacrifices to be offered. The writer of Hebrews expresses this point again later in his book, saying that 'when Christ had offered for all time a single sacrifice for sins, he sat down at the right hand of God... For by a single offering he has perfected for all time those who are being sanctified' (*Heb.* 10:12-14). What can be plainer than this in declaring that Christ has fully paid for all the sins of his people, who believe on his name? John Murray wrote:

Finished! (John 19:30)

From whatever angle we look upon his sacrifice we find its uniqueness to be as inviolable as the uniqueness of his person, of his mission, and of his office. Who is God-man but he alone? Who is great high priest to offer such sacrifice but he alone? Who shed such vicarious blood but he alone? Who entered in once for all into the holy place, having obtained eternal redemption, but he alone?[10]

What is there left for us to do, but trust in Jesus' death for our sins and give him the glory of our hearts: 'Jesus paid it all; all to him I owe / Sin had left a crimson stain; He washed it white as snow.'[11]

The finality of Christ's sacrificial death becomes important when it comes to the matter of present and future sins. Which of my sins did Jesus pay for on the cross? Did Jesus' death only atone for sins I committed before being baptized (as the Roman Catholic Church teaches) or only those sins I committed before I believed (as some unsound Protestant churches teach)? If either of these answers is true, then I must do something to pay for sins I have recently committed, as well as for sins I will commit in the future.

The Roman Catholic doctrines of penance and the mass rely on an incomplete view of Christ's atonement. For Roman Catholics, the mass provides an on-going sacrifice of Christ's blood even today, so the atoning sufferings of Jesus are not finished. Moreover, Rome teaches that one must perform penance—punishments prescribed by a priest in order to be fully restored to God's favour from present sins—so that Christ's atoning death did not complete the work of forgiveness. Unsound Protestants will similarly say that we must ritually confess recent sins in order to be forgiven, and that if a believer in Christ dies with unconfessed sins he or she will not be saved. The problem with these views is that Jesus exclaimed, 'It is finished', when his work was done on the cross. Jesus paid the

[10] John Murray, *Redemption Accomplished and Applied* (Reprint, Edinburgh: Banner of Truth, 2009), p. 48.
[11] Elvina M. Hall (1822-89), 'Jesus Paid It All', 1865.

debt of his people's sins before the vast majority of them were even born. 'I am the good shepherd', he said. 'I know my own and my own know me, just as the Father knows me and I know the Father; and I lay down my life for the sheep' (*John* 10:14-15). When Jesus laid down his life for the sheep he did not lose any of them or leave any of their sins unforgiven. Jesus died not merely for potential believers in general but for the specific, elect persons the Father had given to him from all history to be redeemed by his blood and to enter into that salvation through faith in him alone. Since Christ made a full and final atonement for all his people, those who believe in Christ may know that all their sins are forgiven. As John wrote in his first epistle, 'the blood of Christ cleanses us from all sin' (*1 John* 1:7).

If we are to believe on Jesus' death for our forgiveness, then we must refuse to appeal anywhere else for any type of atonement. Calvin articulates this mandate, especially warning us against the Roman mass or any other supposed means of atonement other than Christ:

> for he who was sent by the Heavenly Father to obtain for us a full acquittal, and to accomplish our redemption, knew well what belonged to his office, and did not fail in what he knew to be demanded of him. It was chiefly for the purpose of giving peace and tranquility to our consciences that he pronounced his word, *It is finished*. Let us stop here, therefore, if we do not choose to be deprived of the salvation which he has procured for us.[12]

Full Atonement, Can It Be?

Jesus' cry, 'It is finished' (*John* 19:30), prompts us lastly to consider the efficacy of his atoning death actually to save his elect people. We may pose this question: Did Jesus effect my atonement with his death on the cross, or did his atoning work depend on my

[12] Calvin, *New Testament Commentaries*, 18:236.

response in faith? Is it possible, in the latter instance, that having died on the cross for sins in general, and having cried out, 'It is finished', Jesus still might not actually have saved anyone, and that his sacrifice was only made of any value when sinners later believed in his gospel? The answer to these questions can be gained by considering the biblical depiction of the design, intent, and actual achievement of Christ's death. This doctrinal distinction is set forth by the competing positions of the Arminian doctrine of general redemption versus the Reformed doctrine of limited atonement (also known as particular redemption).

The difference between these positions is not that one of them limits Christ's atoning work and the other does not. Both general redemption and limited atonement see a limit to Christ's saving death, or else they would embrace the liberal doctrine of universal salvation apart from faith. According to general redemption, Christ's atoning work was unlimited in scope but limited in efficacy. That is, Christ died equally for all persons but did not actually atone for the sins of anyone. Atonement was made effectual only when sinners actually believed. According to limited atonement, or particular redemption, Christ's atoning death was limited in scope, pertaining only to the elect, but unlimited in efficacy. Christ died for his own people, and his atoning death was utterly effectual in paying the debt of their sins, which is why the Holy Spirit was later sent to regenerate these same persons to a saving, personal faith.

The Bible should answer the debate, so we ask, What does the Bible say about the design and intent of Christ's atoning work? One answer was given by the angel who announced Christ's work to Joseph, Mary's betrothed. Joseph was to give the child the name Jesus, 'for he will save *his people* from their sins' (*Matt.* 1:21). This is precisely as was foretold through the prophet Isaiah: 'He was cut off out of the land of the living, stricken for the transgression of *my people*' (*Isa.* 53:8). 'The Son of Man came not to be served but to serve,' Jesus said, 'and to give his life as a ransom *for many*' (*Matt.* 20:28). 'I am the good shepherd', Jesus preached. 'The good shepherd lays down his life for *the sheep*' (*John* 10:11, italics added in all cited verses). Notice that in all of these cases, the objects of Christ's atoning death are not mankind in general, but the elect in particular. This is why the Reformed doctrine teaches the atonement as limited in scope. But, in contrast, the biblical language regarding the saving efficacy of Christ's death is unlimited. John Murray observes:

> The very nature of Christ's mission and accomplishment is involved in this question. Did Christ come to make the salvation of all men possible, to remove obstacles that stood in the way of salvation, and merely to make provision for salvation? Or did he come to save his people?... Did he come to make men redeemable? Or did he come effectually and infallibly to redeem? The doctrine of the atonement must be radically revised if, as atonement, it applies to those who finally perish as well as to those who are the heirs of eternal life.[13]

In light of Jesus' triumphal cry from the cross, 'It is finished', we must surely not believe that the salvation of his people was yet in doubt in any sense, even while we realize that there remained the need for the Holy Spirit to enter into time and bring each of those purchased with Christ's blood to a personal, saving faith. While a sinner can only be saved through faith alone, that faith rests upon the once-for-all finished work of Jesus, when he paid in full the debt of our sins to God's justice and redeemed us into eternal life.

To deny the full efficacy of Christ's atoning death in saving all of those who belong to him is to eradicate the only ground of assurance in salvation. We will never have the peace of assurance

---

[13] Murray, *Redemption*, p. 55.

for our souls so long as we are looking to something in ourselves—something we have done and something that we are doing—as that which finished our redemption. Instead, it is when you realize that even your faith is the outworking of Christ's finished work for you on the cross that you know the solid ground on which your salvation stands.

He Died for Me

Having emphasized the finished nature of Christ's work, we should conclude by noting that the results of his atoning death continue on throughout history. While Christ's work in dying for sins is finished, the work to which he calls us only begins when we look in faith to his cross. In this, too, understanding the finished nature of Christ's work will motivate us to respond in works of service and witness for him.

Indeed, understanding Jesus' finished atonement for our salvation will profoundly influence the psychology of our devotion to him. There are some people who die for a principle, and we admire them for it. Socrates accepted the cup of hemlock for the principle of tacit consent to civic rule. For this act his influence has spread far and wide across the ages. There are others who die for a cause. If we share the cause, we may honour the martyr's name. Nathan Hale has gone down in American history as the revolutionary who declared, 'My only regret is that I have but one life to give for my country.' School children are taught those words even today, and his countrymen remember him with respect. Logically, the doctrine of general redemption places Jesus in these categories, though as the most noble of persons who died for the greatest cause and highest principle possible.

But there is another category that rises far above the rest. Some die for principle and others for a cause. But what about someone who died for me? This calls for a different kind of devotion altogether.

The movie *Saving Private Ryan* tells of a rescue operation immediately after the Allied invasion of Normandy, in June 1944. The War Department learned that three out of four boys in a family named Ryan had died in battle on the same day. The Army's top general ordered that the fourth son be rescued from behind German lines, where he had parachuted on D Day. An elite squad of Army Rangers is assigned to find Private Ryan. Their search leads to a bridge where German tanks are trying to break through Allied lines, and there the squad is destroyed as their quest finally succeeds. As the captain who saved Ryan lies dying on the bridge, surrounded by the bodies of the men from his squad, he draws Ryan close and gasps, 'Earn this. Earn it.' The movie concludes with Ryan, as an old man, returning to the cemetery where the men who died for him were buried. Falling to his knees at Captain Miller's grave, he says to the white plaster cross, 'Every day I think about what you said to me that day on the bridge. I've tried to live my life the best I could. I hope that was enough. I hope that at least in your eyes, I earned what all of you have done for me.' Turning to his wife, who comes up beside him, he stammers, 'Tell me I have led a good life. Tell me I'm a good man.'

Christians, praise God that we are not required to earn what Christ has done for us, nor could we. Jesus did not say, 'Earn this', from the cross, but, 'It is finished.' We receive his death by simple faith, as a gift of God's sovereign love and to the praise of his glorious grace, and we are thus liberated from a Christian life of bondage, trying always to earn our place in God's love.

Yet Jesus' cry, 'It is finished', becomes only the beginning for our faith, which we rest on his full atonement. As we serve Christ from the foundation of his finished work, we offer ourselves not merely for a principle, and not even for a great cause. We live for a person, the Saviour Jesus Christ, whose finished work accomplished our eternal blessing. He died not merely for a principle or even for the greatest of causes. He died for us. So every Christian can, and surely must, say in response: 'I live for him, because he died for me.'

6

WHOM THEY HAVE PIERCED
John 19:31-37

> For these things took place that the Scripture might
> be fulfilled: 'Not one of his bones will be broken.' And
> again another Scripture says, 'They will look on him
> whom they have pierced' (*John* 19:36-37).

WHEN Israel thirsted in the desert, Moses struck the rock
of Horeb with his staff and a stream of water sprang
forth (*Exod.* 17:6). The wilderness was thus a land of death in
which the water of life flowed for the refreshment of God's people.
A noteworthy feature of that episode was that before God told
Moses to strike the rock, he stated, 'Behold, I will stand before you
there on the rock of Horeb' (*Exod.* 17:6). God offered himself to
be struck in the place of his sinful people, with the result that the
waters flowed to give them life. In John 19:34, the apostle John
sees this symbolism fulfilled as the stricken and dead Jesus Christ
is pierced with a soldier's spear 'and at once there came out blood
and water.' It is for this reason that Paul described the rock of
Horeb as a 'spiritual rock', and specified that 'the rock was Christ'
(*1 Cor.* 10:4).

It has been observed that if you squeeze the Gospel of John
hard enough, water will pour out of it. In chapter two, Jesus
ordered servants to fill basins with water and then turned the
water into wine. Jesus was the source of joy at the wedding feast,
giving power for water to become the wine which gladdens men's

hearts (*Psa.* 104:15). In John 4, Jesus sat beside the Samaritan woman at Jacob's well. 'Everyone who drinks of this water will be thirsty again,' he said of the still well water, 'but whoever drinks of the water that I will give him will never be thirsty forever' (*John* 4:13-14). In this way, Jesus presented himself as the fountain of spiritual life for all who believe. Chapter five presented a paralyzed man who lay beside a pool. The pool of Bethesda supposedly had healing powers, but the man could not get into it. Jesus therefore took the place of the pool and granted the man healing. All of these episodes in John's Gospel led up to Jesus' great invitation at the feast of tabernacles: 'If anyone thirsts, let him come to me and drink. Whoever believes in me, as the Scripture has said, "Out of his heart will flow rivers of living water"' (*John* 7:37-38). John explained that Jesus was referring to the gift of God's Spirit after Christ's resurrection, providing eternal life to those who believe. While John 7:37-38 may be seen as a theological high water mark in John's Gospel, the water imagery continues with the blind man washing in the Pool of Siloam (*John* 9:6-7) and Jesus washing the disciples' feet with water (*John* 13:3-10).

How shocking it was, therefore, after this flood of Christ's life-giving water, when Jesus cried from the cross, 'I am thirsty' (*John* 19:28). Here is the full expression of Jesus bearing the curse of God for our sin: the fountain of life dried up in death, the spring of living water cut off at the source as the punishment for sin. Finally, Jesus cried, 'It is finished', and gave up his spirit into the hands of the Father (*John* 19:30), having fully paid the punishment for our sins. What good news it is for Christ's people, then, when John tells us of the spear passing into Jesus' side, as Moses' staff struck the rock of old, and out of his crucified body the flow began again, not just of water but of blood and water together. Out of Jesus' death—by means of his blood—the living water flows once more, and beside this river will grow the tree of life, with fruit for the healing of the nations (*Rev.* 22:2; cf. *Ezek.* 47:12).

No Bones Broken

Jesus was crucified not only on a Friday but on the day of preparation before the Feast of Unleavened Bread. As the dark day drew on, not only was a Sabbath to begin at sundown but a Sabbath that would begin a holy week of sacred feasting. With this in mind, John writes: 'Since it was the day of Preparation, and so that the bodies would not remain on the cross on the Sabbath (for that Sabbath was a high day), the Jews asked Pilate that their legs might be broken and that they might be taken away' (*John* 19:31). The reason for this request was the stricture of Deuteronomy 21:22-23, where the law declared that if an executed man was hung on a tree, 'his body shall not remain all night on the tree, but you shall bury him the same day, for a hanged man is cursed by God' (*Deut.* 21:23). To leave a corpse exposed would defile the holy land, so the priests asked Pilate to hasten the death of those crucified, especially with such a holy Sabbath approaching. We see here yet another example of the Jews' hypocrisy. John Calvin notes: 'In order to a strict observance of their Sabbath, they are careful to avoid outward pollution; and yet they do not consider how shocking a crime it is to take away the life of an innocent man.'[1]

The Roman procedure for hastening the end of a crucifixion, known as the *crurifragium*, involved the smashing of the shin bones with a mallet or iron bar. As a result of this shockingly violent act of supposed mercy, the victim would experience shock and would no longer able to push up and relieve the pressure on his abdomen.

---

[1] John Calvin, *Calvin's Commentaries*, 23 vols. (Grand Rapids, MI: Baker, 1848, reprint 2009), 18:238.

Within a short while, death would arrive by means of asphyxiation. To validate the biblical depiction, in 1968 the skeleton of a man crucified in the first century was found north of Jerusalem. One of the man's legs had been fractured and the other had been broken to pieces.[2]

According to John's eye-witness account, this horrific act was performed on the two men crucified with Jesus: 'the soldiers came and broke the legs of the first, and of the other who had been crucified with him' (*John* 19:32). We know from Luke's Gospel that in this manner one of the two criminals experienced the release of his soul to join Jesus in glory, so that Christ's word was fulfilled: 'Truly, I say to you, today you will be with me in Paradise' (*Luke* 23:43). This believing thief's suffering after his conversion and his horrible death remind us that the gospel does not preserve us from the temporal consequences of sins we commit in this life. J. C. Ryle comments: 'The grace of God and the pardon of sin did not deliver him from the agony of having his legs broken.'[3]

Having administered the *coup de grace* to the two thieves, the soldiers approached the cross of Jesus. John relates: 'But when they came to Jesus and saw that he was already dead, they did not break his legs' (*John* 19:33). With this information, John proves that Jesus truly had died on the cross.

By the time that John was writing his account, it was important to establish Jesus' death against two denials of the gospel. First, there were those who denied that Jesus was truly human and therefore that he actually suffered and died in a human nature and body. This is the heresy of *docetism*, a teaching common to the Gnostic heretics who considered spirit to be pure and all matter to be ignoble. Second, there were then, as now, those who denied

---

[2] Cited by Andreas J. Kostenberger, *John* (Grand Rapids, MI: Baker, 2004), p. 552.
[3] J. C. Ryle, *Expository Thoughts on the Gospels: John,* 3 vols. (Edinburgh: Banner of Truth, 1999), 3:368.

the reality of Jesus' resurrection by means of the 'swoon theory'. Jesus was not raised, sceptics say, because he never died but only fell unconscious on the cross. Jesus was supposedly secreted away and recovered from his wounds so that the early Christians might falsely claim a resurrection. To combat these denials, John cites the most reliable of morticians to bolster the gospel claim of Jesus' true death: Roman legionnaires who had seen corpses of every description and thus were expert judges of whether someone had died or not. So certain were these soldiers, led by a centurion, of Jesus' death that they thought it safe to ignore orders that were given under pain of their own death. There simply was no point breaking the legs of a man who in their certain judgment had undoubtedly already died.

In this providential arrangement, Christians can marvel at the wisdom of God. Our salvation relies so completely on the atonement of Christ that a credible claim against his death on the cross would thoroughly shake, if not destroy, our hope of glory. Gordon Keddie reminds us how easily 'the death of a rock-star like Elvis Presley can become the subject of widespread denial, subsequently supported by supposed sightings by his devoted followers over the years.'[4] With the evidence that John cites, however, neither Christ's devoted followers nor his bitter enemies could ever say 'that He did not really die, and that He was only in a swoon, or fainting fit, or state of insensibility. The Roman soldiers are witnesses that on the centre cross of the three they saw a dead man.'[5]

The Dual Flow of Grace

Perhaps to make sure of Jesus' death or simply as an act of callous disrespect, 'one of the soldiers pierced his side with a spear' (*John* 19:34). We do not know for certain which side was pierced,

---

[4] Gordon J. Keddie, *A Study Commentary on John*, 2 vols. (Darlington: Evangelical Press, 2001), 2:348.
[5] Ryle, *John*, 3:369.

although if the soldier was right-handed it would naturally be Jesus' left side that was penetrated. This is also suggested by the result, which made doubly certain that Jesus was dead: 'at once there came out blood and water' (*John* 19:34).

Numerous sober evangelical commentators view this detail as merely providing one more proof of Jesus' death and urge that to seek a spiritual meaning in the blood and water is unjustified. This view does not account, however, for the importance that the apostle seems to place on this incident, going so far as to provide it special notoriety in his first epistle. There, John states that Jesus 'is he who came by water and blood—Jesus Christ; not by the water only but by the water and the blood' (*1 John* 5:6). Not only does the apostle clearly stress the significance of the blood and water, but these are symbols for which we do not lack clear explanations in the Bible. What insight, then, should we glean from this detail that John considered so important?

First, Christian physicians have sought to diagnose the cause of Jesus' death based on this evidence. Some have argued that Jesus must have died from a physically ruptured heart, with the result that the blood in the heart coagulated so that when the heart was pierced by the spearhead, a darker and a lighter stream of liquid flowed out. Whether or not this explanation is valid, we must remember that Jesus died on a note of triumph, not of a 'broken heart', and that he voluntarily gave up his life by delivering his spirit into the Father's hands (*John* 19:30). Others have persuasively argued that the spear thrust probably penetrated Jesus' pericardium (the fluid sac surrounding the heart), so that blood from the heart flowed out along with water from the open wound.[6]

Second, from the early church many have cited a mystical connection between the blood and water flowing from Christ's

---

[6] See the discussion of these options in William Hendriksen, *Exposition of the Gospel According to John*, New Testament Commentary (Grand Rapids, MI: Baker, 1953), pp. 437-8.

wound and the sacraments of baptism and the eucharist. Augustine wrote that 'Our sacraments have flowed out from Christ's side.'[7] It is very doubtful, however, that John intended any such sacramental understanding of the blood and water of Jesus' wound, especially since there is no record in Scripture of the Lord's Supper and baptism being referred to by these labels.[8]

Third, evangelicals have seen the blood and water as signifying the chief blessings of Christ's sacrificial death. When it comes to the biblical imagery of *blood*, especially in John's writings, the clear and consistent usage pertains to *atonement* for sin, with the result of forgiveness and reconciliation with God (cf. *John* 6:53-54; *1 John* 1:7). Likewise, the *water* rites of the Old Testament all pertain to spiritual *cleansing* from the defiling presence of sin (cf. *John* 3:5, 4:14, 7:38-39). Matthew Henry elaborates:

> Guilt contracted must be expiated by blood; stains contracted must be done away by the water of purification. These two must always go together. You are sanctified, you are justified (*1 Cor.* 6:11). Christ has joined them together and we must not think to put them asunder. They both flowed from the pierced side of our Redeemer... Now was the rock smitten (*1 Cor.* 10:4), now was the fountain opened (*Zech.* 13:1), now were the wells of salvation digged (*Isa.* 12:3). Here is the river, the streams whereof make glad the city of our God.[9]

In emphasizing these two flows from Jesus' pierced side, John directs our faith to Christ's atoning death for both the forgiveness of our sins and the spiritual cleansing of the Holy Spirit, that is, for justification and sanctification. In this way, we see that Jesus died for our great dual problem in sin: our legal problem of guilt and our spiritual problem of corruption. These two problems (and

---

[7] Cited by Keddie, *John*, p. 350.

[8] D.A. Carson, *The Gospel of John* (Grand Rapids, MI: Eerdmans, 1991), p. 624.

[9] Matthew Henry, *Commentary on the Whole Bible*, 6 vols. (Peabody, MA: Hendrickson, n.d.), 5:972.

their solutions) must always be distinguished, just as the blood and water flowing from Christ's side were not mingled, and they must always be kept together, since those whom God justifies in Christ he always sanctifies in Christ. Both result from and flow out of Jesus' sacrificial death for us. Through faith in his cross, we gain these two essential benefits, these twin graces of our salvation, the yield of which is eternal life. This is why the apostle Paul constantly stated that a Christian's salvation is 'in Christ', for from his crucified body flow both justification and sanctification, received by us through faith alone.

Realizing the vital symbolism of the blood and water flowing from the body of Christ, it is no surprise that these have provided the themes for many a beloved Christian hymn. Fanny Crosby was inspired to write:

> Jesus, keep me near the cross:
> There a precious fountain,
> Free to all, a healing stream,
> Flows from Calv'ry's mountain.[10]

Even more familiar to most Christians are the words of Augustus Toplady's famous hymn, *Rock of Ages*, which so clearly relates both justification and sanctification to the crucified body of Jesus:

> Rock of Ages, cleft for me,
> Let me hide myself in Thee;
> Let the water and the blood,
> From thy riven side which flowed,
> Be of sin the double cure,
> Cleanse me from its guilt and power.[11]

---

[10] Fanny J. Crosby (1820-1915), 'Jesus, Keep Me near the Cross', 1869.
[11] Augustus M. Toplady (1740-1778), 'Rock of Ages, Cleft for Me', 1776.

To Fulfil the Scriptures

John's Gospel provides the only record of the piercing of Jesus' side and the flow of blood and water. Therefore he takes pains to establish the credibility of his witness: 'He who saw it has borne witness—his testimony is true, and he knows that he is telling the truth—that you also may believe. For these things took place that the Scripture might be fulfilled' (*John* 19:35-36). In this way, the apostle seems to seek to oblige the legal requirement for two witnesses (cf. *Deut.* 19:15), especially since in the late first century when he was writing, challenges to Jesus' death were already appearing. John points out that he is not alone in citing these events but is joined by the witness of the Old Testament prophets.

First, John points out that the Old Testament foresaw that 'not one of his bones will be broken' (*John* 19:36). This may be a reference to Psalm 34:20, 'He keeps all his bones; not one of them is broken.' This verse serves as a more than adequate testimony to go along with John's account of Jesus' legs not being broken. He is probably thinking as well of the provision in Exodus 12:46 that the Passover lamb's bones must not be broken. In this way, John was not only establishing a witness to his record but also tying in its theological meaning. The fulfilment of the Passover lambs, the blood of which preserved Israelite homes from the angel of death on the eve of the exodus, occurred when Jesus offered his atoning blood for our sins on the cross. As Paul stated, 'For Christ, our Passover lamb, has been sacrificed' (*1 Cor.* 5:7). When John says that he gives his testimony 'that you also may believe' (*John* 19:35), he means that we should confess our need of Christ's blood and appeal to him for atonement and cleansing through faith in his cross.

Second, John notes the prophecy of Zechariah 12:10, 'They will look on him whom they have pierced.' This establishes a biblical witness for the piercing of Jesus' side. But it also provides the theological grid for the meaning of Christ's death. Zechariah saw in Jerusalem's rejection of his own ministry the greater rejection of Israel's true Messiah. He prophesied not only Jesus' death but the preaching of his cross to bring repentance and saving faith to God's people. All this is included in the full statement of Zechariah 12:10: 'I will pour out on the house of David and the inhabitants of Jerusalem a spirit of grace and pleas for mercy, so that, when they look on me, on him whom they have pierced, they shall mourn for him, as one mourns for an only child, and weep bitterly over him, as one weeps over a firstborn.'

The prophet went on to speak of the saving grace that would flow from the preaching of Jesus' death: 'On that day there shall be a fountain opened for the house of David and the inhabitants of Jerusalem, to cleanse them from sin and uncleanness' (*Zech.* 13:1). The ultimate result not only of Jesus' death, opening the fountain of his blood and water, but also of the preaching of his cross, would be the fulfilment of God's ancient purpose in the covenant of grace: 'They will call upon my name, and I will answer them. I will say, "They are my people"; and they will say, "The LORD is my God"' (*Zech.* 13:9). Just as John recorded the day when the blood and water flowed from Jesus' crucified body, and as Zechariah foretold the preaching of the cross for cleansing and salvation, today as the gospel is preached and believed that fountain flows anew so that all who look on him who was pierced, mourn for their sins, and call on him in faith will be forgiven, cleansed, and restored to God for eternal life.

Those who refuse to believe on Jesus' cross will nonetheless look on him whom they pierced when he returns in glory, and they will mourn over their own eternal destruction in the wrath of the triumphant lamb who was slain but now reigns in glory and power. John wrote of this in the opening lines of the book of Revelation: 'Behold, he is coming with the clouds, and every eye will see him, even those who pierced him, and all tribes of the earth will wail on account of him. Even so. Amen' (*Rev.* 1:7).

A Fountain Filled with Blood

I mentioned earlier the names of two hymn writers, Fanny Crosby and Augustus Toplady, who extolled the virtue of the blood and water flowing from Jesus' side. The hymn that is probably best-known for celebrating this theme, 'There Is a Fountain Filled with Blood', was written by the English poet William Cowper. By all accounts Cowper possessed a sensitive, even fragile, disposition, and his mother's death when he was six years old left him mentally unstable. Frequently battling depression, he sought to protect himself by staying busy and keeping his mind diverted. A crisis came, however, when both his father and stepmother died, and then his closest friend was drowned. The result was a mental and emotional collapse, so that Cowper ended up in an insane asylum. At length, he was entrusted to the care of a Christian man, and it was during that time that Cowper came to grasp the meaning of the gospel and the knowledge that Christ had died for him.

Cowper's breakthrough reveals an awareness of the stream of grace that flows through all the Scriptures and comes to us by the wounds of Christ, which he grasped while reading Romans 3:24-25. Paul writes that sinners 'are justified by [God's] grace as a gift, through the redemption that is in Christ Jesus, whom God put forward as a propitiation by his blood, to be received by faith.' Cowper relates: 'Immediately I received strength to believe it and the full beams of the Sun of Righteousness shone upon me. I saw the sufficiency of the atonement He had made, my pardon was sealed in His blood... I could only look up to heaven in silent fear, overwhelmed with love and wonder.'[12]

[12] Cited from Elsie Houghton, *Christian Hymn-Writers* (Bryntirion: Evangelical Press of Wales, 1982), p. 149.

THE DEATH OF THE SAVIOUR

Before long Cowper was able to leave the asylum, his heart cleansed by the fountain of Christ's blood. Throughout his life his mental struggles would continue and he even attempted suicide at various times, yet it was this gospel that led him through a difficult life with light piercing the darkness of his soul. Many of his hymns remain popular still, with titles like *God Moves in a Mysterious Way*, and *O for a Closer Walk with God*. But the hymn for which Cowper is best known gives his testimony to the cleansing blood of Christ, recounting how his burdened heart was set free 'on that day' when the blood of Christ was shed for our sins:

> There is a fountain filled with blood,
> Drawn from Immanuel's veins;
> And sinners, plunged beneath that flood,
> Lose all their guilty stains;
>
> The dying thief rejoiced to see
> That fountain in his day;
> And there have I, as vile as he,
> Washed all my sins away;
>
> E'er since by faith I saw the stream
> Your flowing wounds supply;
> Redeeming love has been my theme,
> And shall be till I die...
>
> Dear dying Lamb, your precious blood
> Shall never lose its power;
> Till all the ransomed church of God
> Be saved, to sin no more.[13]

[13] William Cowper (1731-1800), 'There Is a Fountain Filled with Blood', 1771.

7

A Garden Burial
John 19:38-42

Now in the place where he was crucified there was a garden, and in the garden a new tomb in which no one had yet been laid (*John* 19:41).

THE apostle John opened his Gospel by presenting Jesus as the divine Word who spoke with power at the moment of creation: 'In the beginning was the Word' (*John* 1:1). Creation themes continue throughout John's Gospel, including his reference to the water and blood that flowed from Jesus' side, prompting us to recall the river of life that 'flowed out of Eden to water the garden' (*Gen.* 2:10). We inevitably see as well a creation allusion in John's statement regarding the burial of Jesus' body: 'Now in the place where he was crucified there was a garden, and in the garden a new tomb in which no one had yet been laid' (*John* 19:41).

The apostle does not make an explicit connection between Jesus' burial and the events that took place in the original Garden. Yet it is hard to imagine that John, the author of the Book of Revelation, with its many connections between Old and New Testaments, would have failed to observe a parallel. In the Garden, man came under the judgment of death for sin; Adam's transgression delved a tomb in fear of which his race has ever since lived. Yet through the long ages recorded in the Bible, God had left that tomb empty: mankind had not been destroyed but awaited its deliverer who would lie in that grave for the sins of his people. How fitting it was, then, that Jesus was laid in a garden tomb after his atoning death on the cross. F. B. Meyer writes: 'In a garden man fell; in a garden he was redeemed.' Moreover, by Christ's death the Garden's original design was achieved: 'the death of Christ has sown our world with the flowers of peace and joy and blessedness.'[1]

Crucified, Dead, and Buried

These brief reflections help us to see that Jesus' burial was important to his saving work. The Apostles' Creed acknowledges this importance, reciting that Jesus 'was crucified, dead, and buried.' In John's record of Jesus' death, we have learned that every detail has great meaning, especially as the cross fulfils the Old Testament types and prophecies. What is true of his cross is true of Jesus' tomb: the laying of Jesus' body in the grave was an important and necessary part of his atoning work for our sins.

In 1671, the Puritan John Flavel published a series of forty-two sermons on the death of Jesus, titled *The Fountain of Life*.[2] In Flavel's sermon on the burial of Jesus' body, he listed five reasons why this was an important element of Jesus' saving achievement. The first purpose for Jesus' burial was *to prove the reality of his death*.

So vital is the death of Jesus to the Christian doctrine of salvation that this event has been an obvious target for those who would oppose the gospel. Writing his Gospel late in the first century, John was familiar with denials of Jesus' true humanity and especially of his actual, physical death. Therefore, Flavel writes, 'since our eternal life is wrapt up in Christ's death, it can never be too firmly established.'[3] If it was not already certain that Jesus was dead after the Roman soldiers certified his death and drove a spearhead into

---

[1] F. B. Meyer, *John: The Life of Love* (Old Tappan, NJ: Fleming Revell, 1987), p. 383.
[2] In John Flavel, *The Works of John Flavel*, 6 vols. (1820; repr. Edinburgh: Banner of Truth, 1968).
[3] Flavel, *Works*, 1:456.

his torso, Jesus' burial placed the matter beyond dispute. John tells us that Joseph of Arimathea and Nicodemus packed Jesus' body with spices and wrapped it in cloths (*John* 19:40; 20:7). After Jesus' burial in this manner, there is no reasonable doubt as to the fact of his death.

Jesus' burial was also important *to certify the truth of his resurrection*, since it was necessary to establish that his body had been securely kept. This was surely one of God's aims in providing a previously unknown disciple to claim Jesus' body and place it in his own nearby tomb (see *Matt.* 27:60). Since Joseph's grave was a new tomb and had never been used, there was no possibility of confusion as to the body. Since the tomb was cut out of rock, there was no possibility for a secret entryway by which Jesus' followers might have stolen the body. Moreover, since Jesus' opponents asked Pilate to seal and set a guard on the grave, the security of his body was as safe as was conceivably possible (see *Matt.* 27:62-66). In their joint discussions regarding Jesus' burial, not only his disciples but also the Roman soldiers, Pontius Pilate, and the Jewish priests and Pharisees gave joint testimony to his death and to the security of his body in the grave.

A third reason for Jesus' burial was *to fulfil the types and prophecies* of the Old Testament. Just as Jonah was buried within the great fish, Jesus said that he would emerge from the grave on the third day with a gospel of salvation (*Matt.* 12:40). Jesus pointed out not merely that Jonah prefigured his death and resurrection, but also that Jonah's ministry of salvation to the wicked Gentiles of Nineveh prefigured Christ's resurrection power to spread the gospel to all nations. 'The men of Nineveh will rise up at the judgment with this generation and condemn it,' he preached, 'for they repented at the preaching of Jonah, and behold, something greater than Jonah is here' (*Matt.* 12:41).

THE DEATH OF THE SAVIOUR

An additional prophecy said, 'they made his grave with the wicked and with a rich man in his death' (*Isa.* 53:9). This prophecy, so unlikely in view of the other circumstances of Jesus' execution, was fulfilled to the letter in the burial of his body in Joseph of Arimathea's grave. We are here reminded not only of the honour that God ascribed to his Son, not willing for his body to be callously disposed of, but also of the certain fulfilment of all the Bible's prophecies and promises, especially those pertaining to Christ's second coming.

Fourth, Jesus was buried in the grave *to complete his humiliation*. The grave was, writes Flavel, 'the lowest step he could possibly descend to in his abased state.'[4] If the depth of Christ's love for us can be measured by the humiliation he endured for our salvation, then the grave bears the full testimony of our Saviour's devotion to his people. Jesus was born to die for sin, and the Son of God who humbled himself to be fashioned as a baby in the womb of the virgin Mary humbled himself even further by submitting his body to be laid in the grave. 'You lay me in the dust of death,' says Psalm 22:15. John began his Gospel by saying, 'In him was life and the life was the light of men' (*John* 1:4). How great is the love of Jesus, then, to endure the darkness of death so that we might be saved from it.

Fifth, Jesus was buried so as *to conquer death and the grave* for us. Flavel exults: 'The great end and reason of his interment was *the conquering of death* in its own dominion and territories; which victory over the grave furnished the saints with that triumphant... song of deliverance, "O death! Where is thy sting? O grave! Where is thy destruction?"'[5] Jesus entered the grave to break its power by his resurrection, opening the gates

[4] Flavel, *Works*, 1:457.
[5] Flavel, *Works*, 1:457.

for his people who like Jesus will remain in their coffins not one minute longer than God appoints. Flavel concludes:

> Death is a dragon, the grave its den; a place of dread and terror; but Christ goes into its den, there grapples with it, and for ever overcomes it; disarms it of all its terror; and not only makes it to cease to be *inimical*, but to become exceeding *beneficial* to his saints; a bed of rest, and a perfumed bed; they do but go into Christ's bed, where he lay before them. For these ends he must be buried.[6]

The Burial of a King

Having considered the purpose and design of Christ's burial, we should attend to the details of Jesus' interment. First, we should note that Jesus received a private, not a public, burial. Few people seem to have attended to the interment of God's Son. This accords with the general lack of honour granted to Jesus by the kingdom of this world. Isaiah said, 'He was despised and rejected by men' (*Isa.* 53:3), and this continued in the disposing of Jesus' body. Jesus had told Pilate, 'My kingdom is not of this world' (*John* 18:36), and accordingly the world ignored the King of heaven's funeral. Once the world had removed Jesus, it no longer had any concern for him, just as the world today permits no more than sentimental interest in Jesus. Israel's Messiah was therefore buried without pomp, but not without God's care for his body.

The Roman preference would have been for Jesus' body to remain on the cross to decompose and provide fodder for the carrion birds. Since this was contrary to Jewish law, the Romans permitted them to bury the bodies of crucified victims. The Jews, however, did not permit the remains of criminals to desecrate their graveyards, so Jesus' body would probably have been disposed of in the burning dumpyard outside the city, the name of which,

---

[6] Flavel, *Works*, 1:457.

Gehenna, became symbolic for the fires of God's wrath in hell. The request of Joseph of Arimathea to bury Jesus body delivered him from this indignity.[7]

For all the public disinterest, John provides details that show that Jesus was buried in a manner fitting for a king: 'Nicodemus also, who earlier had come to Jesus by night, came bringing a mixture of myrrh and aloes, about seventy-five pounds in weight. So they took the body of Jesus and bound it in linen cloths with the spices, as is the burial custom of the Jews' (*John* 19:39-40).

Myrrh was a fragrant resin used by the Egyptians in embalming the dead. The Jews mixed it with aloe, an aromatic powder. Their use was not to embalm the dead, since the Jews did not remove any organs in their burial preparations, but simply to combat the smell of the body's decomposition. Nicodemus brought an enormous amount of this spiced mixture, which scholars today consider to have exceeded sixty-five pounds. John describes the customary Jewish preparation of the body, with strips of cloth laden with myrrh and aloes wound around Jesus' body. More spice would have been packed around and under the body as well.

So staggering is the amount of spices cited by John, far exceeding that normally required, that some scholars have accused John of error or exaggeration. They fail to realize that John is continuing the royal theme that has pervaded his account of the cross. When Asa, one of the great kings of Judah, died, they buried him in a newly cut tomb 'on a bier that had been filled with various kinds of spices prepared by the perfumer's art' (*2 Chron.* 16:14). Herod the Great's funeral procession included five hundred servants bearing spices. Later in the first century, a ruler named Onkelos burned

[7] R. C. Sproul, *John* (Orlando, FL: Reformation Trust, 2009), p. 375.

eighty pounds of spices at the funeral of the rabbi Gamaliel. When asked the reason, he answered 'Is not Rabbi Gamaliel far better than a hundred kings?' Joseph and Nicodemus were contemporaries of Onkelos and Gamaliel, and in their manner of burying Jesus they were declaring, 'Is not Jesus far greater than all other kings?'[8]

Tombs were cut out of the solid sandstone that surrounded Jerusalem and typically included an inner chamber where the body (or bodies) would be lain in death. The doorway consisted of a groove into which a heavy stone had been fitted to block the entryway. Normally, the body would lie on its slab until it fully decomposed, at which point the bones would be placed into an ornate box called an ossuary. John notes that the time for Jesus' burial was short 'because of the Jewish day of Preparation' (*John* 19:42). At sundown the holy Sabbath would arrive, leaving Joseph and Nicodemus little time to prepare. By God's providence, Joseph's own newly-cut tomb was nearby, so this ruler who had been a secret disciple now had the honour of placing Jesus' body in his own grave. We praise our heroes today by burying them with honours in our national cemetery, and like the godly kings of old, Jesus 'was buried with his fathers in the city of David' (*2 Kings* 15:7). Jesus' humiliation called for him to die for the sins of others and be buried in another man's tomb. Having completed his work in death, his exaltation to glory thus began even in the grave. Since Jesus' body was preserved by God from suffering decay (*Psa.* 16:10), his tomb smelled only of sweet fragrance as it waited for the resurrection morning. F. W. Krummacher comments:

Who does not perceive that even in the circumstances of His interment, the overruling hand of God has interwoven for our con-

---

[8] George R. Beasley-Murray, *John*, Word Biblical Commentary 36 (Waco, TX: Word, 1987), p. 359.

solation a gentle testimony, that His only-begotten Son had well accomplished the great task which He was commissioned to perform?[9]

Comfort for Christians

The burial of Jesus is of great interest to Christians not only because of what it says about our Lord but because unless Jesus should first return each of us must also enter the grave.

The burial of Jesus informs us of the biblical understanding of the body even in death and has thus shaped the burial practices of Christians from the earliest days of the church. According to the Bible, a person does not merely inhabit the body but the body is part of the person, even though death effects a separation of body and soul. The souls of believers depart in death for the presence of God in heaven (*2 Cor.* 5:8) and their bodies are placed in the grave to await the resurrection. Notice, in this respect, that while verse 40 says that they bound 'the body of Jesus', verse 42 states that 'they laid Jesus' into the tomb. In other words, the body of Jesus was still Jesus. This shows that Jesus retained his full humanity even in death and it argues that our bodies, even after the soul has departed, remain part of ourselves and ought to be treated with dignity and honour.

Because of the Bible's teaching on the body and on death, Christians have almost universally practised the burial of the body rather than cremation.[10] Only recently has the practice of cremation spread among professing Christians. The primary reason seems to be financial, yet this trend testifies to the decline of biblical thinking among believers. In the Old Testament, the

---

[9] F. W. Krummacher, *The Suffering Saviour* (Edinburgh: Banner of Truth, 1856, reprint, 2004), p. 443.

[10] For a thorough discussion of the biblical background pertaining to burial and cremation, see David W. Jones, 'To Bury or Burn? Toward an Ethic of Cremation', in *Journal of the Evangelical Theological Society*, 53:2 (June 2010), pp. 335-47.

burning of bodies was considered a sign of divine judgment and a portent of the torments of hell, whereas the godly were buried with honour as was the body of Christ (e.g. *Josh.* 7:25-26; *1 Kings* 13:2, 16:18; *2 Kings* 23:4).

It is true that with time a buried body will decay into much the same condition as those consumed in fire, but Christians have declined to treat the body as disposable remains, instead committing it to God's care with reverence. Cremation would seem to pose no barrier to God's ability to raise the dead, and we should note that the Bible never explicitly commands burial versus cremation. Yet our view of the afterlife will always influence how we handle the bodies of those who have died. Whereas cremation results from a pagan view of the body and the afterlife in which matter is released into spirit, Christian burial is shaped by the hope of a bodily resurrection. Paul writes: 'the Lord himself will descend from heaven with a cry of command, with the voice of an archangel, and with the sound of the trumpet of God. And the dead in Christ will rise first' (*1 Thess.* 4:16). This description urges us to honour, preserve, and even dedicate real estate to the bodies of those who having died in Christ now await the resurrection of their bodies in the morning of the new creation. John Flavel summarizes:

> There is a respect due to [Christian bodies], as they are the temples wherein God hath been served, and honoured by those holy souls that once dwelt in them; as also upon the account of their relation to Christ, even when they lie by the walls; and the glory that will one day put upon them, when they shall be changed, and made like unto Christ's glorious body.[11]

Second, the burial of Jesus provides Christians with great consolations against the fear of death. For by lying in Joseph's tomb, Jesus has entered the grave in advance of all his people. God told

[11] Flavel, *Works*, 1:461.

Jacob not to be afraid to go down to Egypt, since 'I myself will go down with you to Egypt, and I will also bring you up again' (*Gen.* 46:3-4). Christians likewise should not fear the grave, since God will be with us there and has promised to raise us from it into glory.

Flavel lists several reasons why Christians face the grave without fear. First, 'the grave *received*, but could not *destroy* Jesus Christ: death swallowed him, as the whale did Jonah his type, but could not digest him when it had swallowed him, but quickly delivered him up again.'[12] Christ entered the grave not as a private person but as the covenant head of all his people. Just as his death exhausted the curse of sin against believers, so also his entering the grave has claimed it as the sleep chamber for those awaiting the resurrection. His resurrection is the ground of our certain hope to triumph over death and the grave. Paul exclaims, 'Christ has been raised from the dead, the firstfruits of those who have fallen asleep' (*1 Cor.* 15:20).

Second, Christians gain consolation knowing that just as our souls belong to Jesus through faith, our bodies are united to him even in death. 'Precious in the sight of the LORD is the death of his saints' (*Psa.* 116:15), says the Bible, and our bodies are likewise precious to God even in the grave. Proverbs 14:32 says, 'the righteous finds refuge in his death', and our refuge is the union of our bodies and souls to the Saviour. In death, David sang, 'I will fear no evil, for you are with me; your rod and your staff, they comfort me' (*Psa.* 23:4).

Third, Christ has conquered death and the grave so that its curse is removed from his people. It is for this reason that David wrote of passing through 'the valley of the shadow of death' (*Psa.* 23:4). Christians do not enter death as a final destination, but we pass through death into eternal glory, and even death itself has become in Christ no more than a shadow. Matthew Henry writes, 'There is

---

[12] Flavel, *Works*, 1:463.

no substantial evil in it; the shadow of a serpent will not sting nor the shadow of a sword kill."[13]

Finally, Jesus reached the final depth of his humiliation in death and burial, yet his exaltation began even in the hurried minutes of his funeral. So also will the laying of our bodies in the grave begin our transition into glory. Charles Spurgeon writes:

> The grave—what is it? It is the bath in which the Christian puts the clothes of his body to have them washed and cleansed. Death— what is it? It is the waiting room where we robe ourselves for immortality; it is the place where the body, like Esther, bathes itself in spices that it may be fit for the embrace of its Lord. Death is the gate of life; I will not fear to die, then.[14]

Isaiah's prophecy said that while Jesus died in the company of the wicked he would be buried together with the rich (*Isa.* 53:9). So it is that riches and glory await all who die in Christ, since in him we have died to sin and been raised through faith into never-ending life with God.

The Urgency of Trusting in Jesus

When man sinned in the Garden, he dug a grave where either he or Jesus must die under God's judgment, and so it is for every sinner even today. Therefore, Christ concluded his earthly ministry by entering a garden and taking residence in the grave. There, he remedied the enmity with God brought on by Adam's sin and ours, and from his grave Jesus restores his people to fellowship and dominion with God. How urgent it is, therefore, that we should be joined to Christ through faith and that he should have entered that grave for us personally. Flavel notes:

[13] Matthew Henry, *Commentary*, 3:259.
[14] C. H. Spurgeon, 'The Tomb of Christ', in *The New Park Street Pulpit*, Vol. 1 (London: Passmore & Alabaster, 1856), p. 140.

THE DEATH OF THE SAVIOUR

The grave is a terrible place to them that are out of Christ; death is the Lord's sergeant to arrest them; the grave is the Lord's prison to secure them... Death there reigns over them in its full power (*Rom.* 5:14)... But the case of the saints is not so; the grave (thanks be to our Lord Jesus Christ!) is a privileged place to them, whilst they sleep there; and when they awake, it will be with singing.[15]

What a great privilege it was for Joseph and Nicodemus, those two belated disciples, to bear Jesus' body into the grave where he would conquer death. What a privilege it is for us to bear his good news into a world held captive by fear of death. What an urgent matter it is for every soul to believe on Jesus Christ, placing our sins on his cross and our hopes in his resurrection life, taking up by faith the Christian song of rejoicing and praise:

> O death, where is your victory?
> O death, where is your sting?
> The sting of death is sin,
>   and the power of sin is the law.
> But thanks be to God, who gives us
>   the victory through our Lord Jesus Christ.

> (*1 Cor.* 15:55-57)

[15] Flavel, *Works*, 1:464.

Also available from
The Banner of Truth Trust

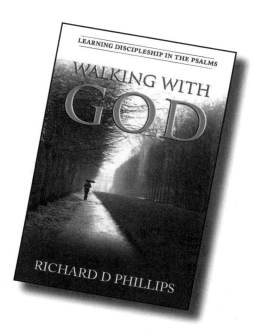

Walking With God:
Learning Discipleship in the Psalms
Richard D. Phillips

We all want to find happiness in this life, but do we know where true happiness is to be found? Richard Phillips believes the book of Psalms has the answer to this pressing question. Beginning with 'The Way of Blessing' set out in Psalm 1, he takes us on a tour of twelve choice Psalms, drawing out many practical lessons aimed at encouraging those who would be better disciples of our Lord Jesus Christ. Other chapter titles include, 'How to Praise the Lord', 'How to Pray', 'From Fear to Faith', 'Pathway to Joy', and 'Spiritual Recovery'.

ISBN: 978-0-85151-895-4 182pp. Paperback